A HISTORY OF ORGIES

A History of Orgies

by Burgo Partridge

Crown Publishers, Inc., New York

CONTENTS

PREFACE

AN orgy is an organized blowing-off of steam; the expulsion of hysteria accumulated by abstinence and restraint, and as such tends to be of an hysterical or cathartic nature.

Every kind of restraint produces its tensions. Man is in the awkward position of possessing both civilized and animal inclinations which have somehow to be reconciled, usually to the disadvantage of the latter, but increasing pressure cannot be withstood for ever, and so, from every kind of tension there is a release—the orgy. Many orgies would not be generally described as such. Wars are, in one sense, an extreme and disagreeable form, farther down the scale come quarrels at cocktail-parties, the practical jokes of stockbrokers, minor marital infidelities—one need not elaborate.

In this book orgies of a sexual character or origin only will be included; this, both because of their superior interest for everybody, and because of the difficulties of recognizing and defining some orgies of other kinds as such.

The orgy serves the useful purpose, not only of providing relief from tension caused by abstinence, necessary or unnecessary, but also of rearousing by contrast an appetite for the humdrum temperances which are an inevitable part of everyday life. Hence it has been used by such very different groups as the peoples of Ancient Greece, and (unwillingly), the medieval Christian Church.

There is, however, another kind of orgy, that of the individual. This is not, in fact essentially is not, organized or condoned by the state or by society, since it arises from the equation by the individual, of the society or state with the sense of confinement and restriction which afflicts him. This equation is often justified, on the other hand it is sometimes mistaken or inaccurately thought out.

These latter are perhaps the more interesting and less repetitive: the rebel is a more intriguing figure than the conformist, and in this particular field of study it is the latter who has received the greater attention. If one of them is treated at disproportionate length, it is hoped that the motives of the author will be understood.

Both kinds of orgy, the conformist and the rebel, can be reduced to the same principle—an escape from intolerable tension. One is likely to be successful, since it attacks the true root of the trouble, and if not accompanied by too-intense feelings of guilt and self-disgust will probably continue to function smoothly.

The other kind, that of the rebel, may also, providing the equation of oppression with society is correct, be satisfactory— but even so, the orgiast is likely to be a lonely and not altogether happy man—he will probably have over-reacted and have been driven to a degree of licence not indigenous to him.

The first two chapters deal with orgiasts of the conformist kind, but it was from one or other of these two very different patterns that subsequent 'rebels' tended to choose. Hence, it is important that the Greek and Roman natures should be born in mind, and the path for some attempt at ethical evaluation laid open.

ONE

THE GREEKS

To those who like to imagine that achievement and success in life depend on subtlety and sophistication, and that intelligence and naïvety are incompatibles, an examination of the Greek way of life and thought brings an enlightening surprise.

The Greek nation achieved wonders of art, thought and political theory which were not rivalled, if indeed they have ever been equalled, for over a dozen centuries. Nevertheless, in their practical everyday life the Greeks based their behaviour and ideals on an extraordinarily simple and sensual Hedonism. They differed from most modern people in that they were immune to the disease which afflicts so many people today, the fixation on one target or object in life to the exclusion of all others, and the semi-obsessional pursuit of this object with corresponding undervaluation of other alternative possibilities.

The Greeks were idealists and enthusiasts for everything connected with living, youth was regarded as an especially dear possession, and the joys of youth the greatest happiness. Beauty and love above all belonged to the pleasures of life desired by them, and these were proclaimed by the poets as ideal. Health was to be valued as without it happiness could not easily exist, and happiness was the only end of life. A cheerful enjoyment of life *in general* was judged by Solon to be a possession worth striving for. Everywhere, in literature, and in the lives of particular men, the efforts of the Greeks indicated ideal wishes, not for money alone, or for reputation alone, or for any lopsided condition in human life. The culture of the Greeks is entirely a song in praise of pleasure, and the nature of that pleasure was an intense and ingenuous sensuality. At all intellectual levels the people recognized the essential part played by voluptuous materialism in human affairs. Not until he was an old man did Sophocles produce the well-known remark that old age is to be praised since it sets us free from the servitude of sensuality. The Greek attitude towards desire was very different.

The poet Simonides asks, 'Would the life of mortals be delightful without sensual happiness? Is not even the life of the blessed gods unenviable without this?'

The Greek gods, who perhaps reflect the nature of their human children more closely than in any other civilization, are subject also to the desires and pleasures of the flesh.

In the eighth book of the *Odyssey* there is a particularly significant scene in which Aphrodite abandons herself to the illicit joys of love with Ares, the sun-god. Her husband, the limping Hephaestus, summons all the other gods to witness the adultery of the two deities, and, after watching this spectacle; 'but to Hermes said the lord Apollo, son of Zeus, "Hermes, son of Zeus, messenger, giver of good things, wouldst thou in sooth be willing, even though ensnared with strong bonds, to lie on a couch by the side of golden Aphrodite?" Then the messenger, Argeiphontes, answered him: "Would that this might befall, lord Apollo, thou archer god . . . that thrice as many bonds inextricable might clasp me about and ye gods, aye, and all the goddesses too, might be looking on, but that I might sleep by the side of golden Aphrodite" so spake he, and laughter arose among the immortal gods.' Not a word of moral reprobation, only laughter and delight form the comment of the Greek gods on this mockery of married fidelity by the goddess of love herself. The rules governing sexual behaviour, such as they were, had only civil force; the Christian idea of 'sin' was the concept of a later civilization.

Megacleides, the historian, blames the poets for laying too much emphasis upon the labours and privations of Heracles, the Greek national hero, during his association with mankind. He points out that Heracles took the greatest pleasure in sensuality, married a large number of women and begat innumerable children. He enjoyed eating and bathing, and throughout Greece a kind of specially soft bed bore Heracles as a trade mark. Megacleides attacks the poets not merely for carelessly omitting one important aspect of the life of Heracles but of offering an actual insult to him in doing so.

None the less, the Greeks were too well balanced a people to give themselves up to perpetual riot and feasting. They recognized that chastity is an essential aperitif to impudicity, and that erotic joys, no matter how delicious, cannot be indulged in all the time. All the same, sensuality was regarded by the Greeks as a serious subject and treated as such by the writers.

Atheneaus of Nauclia, in the twelfth chapter of his *Deipnosophists*, discusses the idea of pleasure theoretically, and then goes on to give examples drawn from various peoples, beginning with the Persians, informing us how each of them knew how to fill life with feasting and debauchery, and following this up with a list of men renowned for their sensual life.

The Persian king, according to Heracleides, had a harem of three hundred women, 'these sleep throughout the day in order to stay awake at night, but at night they sing and play on harps continually while the lamps burn; and the king takes his pleasure of them as concubines.' These women used also to accompany the king on his hunting expeditions.

The Lydians, according to Xanthus, used to castrate not only boys, but also girls, to be employed as eunuchs in the palaces of the great.

The inhabitants of Sybaris introduced hot baths and were the first people to make use of chamber pots at banquets.

In the city of Tarentum, in lower Italy, according to Clearchus, the people, after they had 'acquired strength and power . . . progressed to such a point of luxury as to have the skin of their entire bodies made smooth, and so inaugurated the practice of removing the hair for all other peoples. All the men wore a transparent cloak with purple border . . . garments which today are a refinement of women's fashions. But later, blindly led by luxury into outrage, they uprooted Carbina, a city of the Iaphygians, made the boys, girls and women in their prime gather in the temple of Carbina, and there got up a spectacle, exposing their bodies naked for all to gaze at by day; and anyone who wished, leaping like wolves upon a herd into this wretched group, could feast his lust upon the beauty of the victims there gathered.' The gods apparently disapproved of this particular form of sensuality, for presently the debauchees were struck by lightning.

It must be here admitted that, before launching into a panegyric of the Greek way of life one should consider the treatise of Heracleides Ponticus, a pupil of Plato and a philosopher in his own right. In his essay 'On pleasure' it is affirmed that luxury in the conduct of life is a prerogative of the governing classes, toil and boredom falling to the lot of the slave and the poor. All those who value sensuality and luxury are superior in character to those who do not. The Athenians developed into an heroic people because of, not in spite of, their sybaritic lives. The point of view expressed in the first part of the treatise is a disagreeable one, and although the extent to which it was reflected in actual behaviour is to be very much doubted, it cannot be forgotten that the slaves and the poor were sometimes both mentally and actually excluded from the human race. It is possible that the Greeks may have taken a slightly *too* religious view of pleasure, and have held that anything which ever had or ever could cause joy, was, whatever the other circumstances, good. The Hedonism of the Greeks was not the Hedonism of J. S. Mill.

To return to the list of Athenaeus. The inhabitants of Colophon had, according to him, never seen the sunset or sunrise in their lives, since when the sun rose they were still drunk, and when it set they were drunk again.

Sardanapalus, the last king of Assyria, wrote the following epitaph on himself: 'I have been a king, and as long as I saw the light of the sun, I have eaten, drunk, and done homage to the joys of love, knowing that the lifetime of men is only short and subject to much change and misfortune, and that others will reap the benefit of the possessions that I leave behind me. For this reason I let no day pass without living in this manner.' His philosophy was that of the author of Ecclesiastes, the conclusion to which it led him was somewhat different.

Aristobalus writes of a monument to Sardanapalus in Anchiale. The right hand of the statue was portrayed as being in the act of snapping the fingers. The inscription was as follows: 'Sardanapalus, son of Anacyndaraxes, built Anchiale and Tarsus in a single day. Eat, drink and play for other things are not worth that much.'

Lysias, the orator, tells the following story of Alcibiades and Axiochus: '(they) sailed forth together to the Hellespont, and married together in Abydus, the two of them, Medontis of Abydus, with whom they cohabited. Later a daughter was born to them, of whom they declared they could not tell whose child she was. But when she became marriageable, they cohabited with her also; whenever Alcibiades enjoyed possession of her he would say she was the daughter of Axiochus, but when Axiochus did so he would say she was the daughter of Alcibiades.'

Clearchus relates of Dionysius the Younger, the Tyrant of Sicily, the following tale:

'When Dionysius reached his mother-city Locris, he had the largest house in the city filled with wild thyme and roses, then sent for the young women of Locris one after the other, stripped himself and them naked, and rolled on the bed with them, practising every kind of obscenity imaginable. Shortly afterwards, when the insulted husbands and fathers had got the wife and children of Dionysius into their power, they forced them to commit indecencies before the eyes of all, and abandoned themselves to every kind of conceivable debauchery. After they had satisfied their desire they drove needles under their fingernails and put them to death.'

Strabo repeats the same story, adding that after the room had been prepared, doves with clipped wings were released in the hall and these the naked girls were compelled to catch, some of them being forced to wear sandals which were not a pair, on one foot a low, on the other a high heel.

Demetrius of Phalerum, Governor of Athens for many years, was said to have 'secret orgies with women, and nightly amours with young men'; he took considerable pride in his personal appearance, dyed his hair an improbable shade of blond, and made up his face.

The philosophy that pleasure is the true object of life was supported by an entire philosophical school, that of Aristippus, who in his own life demonstrated his faith in his philosophy, and had as his mistress Laïs, a prominent hetaira.

Most of the men listed by Athenaeus are to be pitied. They belong to the category of rebels, and their orgies represent an attempt to escape from something bigger and more inescapable than the mere restraints of convention. These men were individuals only, not representatives of the race, for the Greeks, it should not be forgotten, achieved an attitude towards sexual matters not since equalled in its realistic sanity. Hedonists they may have been, but they were wise enough to know that pleasure of a purely sensual kind palls soon enough if not alternated with periods of rest and abstinence.

Many other examples could be and will be given of extremes of luxury and debauchery in the Hellenic world. First, one should look briefly at the Greek concept of marriage, and of the attitude towards women in general. Having looked at the 'mother-woman' one is in a position to compare the 'whore-woman' and to pass from the Greek attitude towards hetairae, to religion, erotic festivals, the games, orgies of the 'social' kind, and to the startling ubiquity of homosexuality.

The nature of Greek marriage and the position occupied by women in the Hellenic world is exceedingly difficult to assess in the form of comprehensible images at this distance of time; and if one attempts to do so by modern standards a mass of apparently contradictory material presents itself to his confused mind.

In the first place, there is the undoubtedly very varied position of women in different parts of Greece. The general impression is that women led a life of semi-oriental seclusion and restraint; but whilst some were shut up in the gynaekonitis under lock and key, and guarded by a Molossian hound, in Lydia it was taken for granted if unmarried girls paid for their clothes and earned a dowry by prostitution.

In spite of this last example, there is little doubt that as regards actual physical freedom Greek women would appear intolerably restrained through modern eyes. The Greek view was that the place of women was in the home, her function as an animal being housewife and mother. She had no place in intellectual life, nor was she free to roam unaccompanied in the streets. This should not, however incredible it may seem, be necessarily taken to indicate a view of women as inferior beings, but only of them as different beings, with a different, although by no means inferior, function in life to men. If adultery in husbands was more tolerated than similar action on the part of a wife, this was because the Greeks recognized the polygamous instincts of men as opposed to the, theoretically at least, more monogamous inclinations of women. Extra-marital sexual adventure was tolerated so long as the woman was not of free birth or the wife of another man. The debauchment of a mother or a wife was a different matter. Into all this one can see creeping a strange resemblance to the Victorian view of life; the same sort of division into respectable women and courtesans—the mother/whore division. The difference between the two societies lies in the fact that the Victorian viewpoint started with the precept that sex was something that could not be inflicted on, or satisfactorily enjoyed with, a member of one's own class. The Greek did not. Greek marriage was, in spite of the apparent slavery of the women, a more civilized and satisfactory estate than the Victorian. Divorce could be obtained on grounds of mutual incompatibility, a situation comparing favourably with the present legal position. Above all, there existed between husband and wife a real affection, a co-operation in fulfilling different functions in life, and a state of mutual admiration for each other's performances. Of this there is ample testimony in literature. Let anybody who thinks that because the Greek woman was confined to the world of the household she was a slave, and that Greek men treated their women as such, read the description of the parting between Hector and Andromache in the *Iliad* of Homer.

That infidelity should occur on the part of the husband and, less frequently, of the wife, was, if regrettable to present-day morality, in accordance with the Hedonistic view of life and less endangering to the unity of the marriage for this very reason. The Greeks realized what hardly anybody else appeared to observe during most of the ensuing two thousand years, that a passing lust for A is not incompatible with a more permanent love for B, and light-hearted representation of the devices employed by Greek wives to deceive their husbands appear in comedy. Moreover, the Greeks realized what the Victorians did not, that the restraints imposed on married women, whether desirable and justifiable or not, were imposing a strain, and one which it would be as well to alleviate from time to time. In practice and on the emotional level, Greek women may have experienced jealousy and rage at the adventures of their husbands with the hetairae. They would not have been human if they had not. Rationally, the principle was a widely accepted one and, if savouring of cynicism, prudent.

The girls who provided this alternative to married inter-course were not regarded as mere safety-valves, even though this is what they undoubtedly were. With the naïvety displayed by the Greeks in all sexual matters they were treated much more like priestesses of the Hedonistic cult. The difference between the position of hetairae in Greece and prostitutes in modern civilization is manifested vividly and startlingly by two examples. The inhabitants of Thespiae, a town to which Phryne, a famous hetaira, had presented a magnificent statue of Eros, returned the compliment by commissioning Praxiteles to execute a gilded statue of her. This was set up in the square, between the statues of King Archiadamus and Philippus, where no one took any offence at it. On the tombstone of Kallirrohe of Byzantium appears the following inscription: 'I was a harlot in the city of Byzantium and granted to all the love that I sold. I am Kallirrohe experienced in all the arts of voluptuousness. Lashed by the stings of love Thomas has placed this epitaph on my grave and thereby showed what passion dwelt in his soul; his heart melted and became as softened as wax.'

The hetairae, who were regarded as superior to brothel-dwelling prostitutes, and whose charges reflected this opinion, were admired for intellectual qualities as well as physical, although how far one hindered an objective assessment of the other may be the object of cynical disbelief.

They were frequently enlisted to lend their support to the worship of Aphrodite. At Corinth, a town constantly mentioned in Greek literature as being renowned for the debauchery of its inhabitants ('of the wantonness and licentiousness of life in this metropolis of ancient trade, so wealthy and so favoured by nature, it would be difficult to give an account that should err by exaggeration,' says Licht). Or, according to the invaluable Athenaeus: 'There has existed a custom, that the city, when it offers prayers to Aphrodite in a great procession, draws as large a number of hetairae as possible into it, and these also pray to the goddess and are present at the sacrifice and sacrificial feast.' Temple prostitution took place at a number of places, notably Corinth, Cyprus and Abydos. To these temples the victor at the Olympic games would sometimes make a present of girls.

Strabo wrote of the temple of Aphrodite Porne at Corinth: 'The temple of Aphrodite was so wealthy, that it was able to keep more than a thousand hetairae who were dedicated to the goddess by men and women. For the sake of these girls strangers crowded thither so that the city became rich thereby.' (The very fact that Aphrodite, as well as being the goddess of love, could also appear as 'Aphrodite the Whore', demonstrates the lack of illusion about human nature in the Greek world.)

Lucian gives an account of the temple at Byblos: 'At Byblos I also saw the great temple of Aphrodite and became acquainted with the orgies that are common there. The inhabitants believe that the death of Adonis when he was killed by a boar, took place in their country, and in memory thereof they beat their breasts every year and lament, and great mourning prevails throughout the country. When they have finished with beating and lamentation, they perform the obsequies of Adonis, and on the following day they pretend that he has wakened to life, place him in heaven, and shave their heads like the Egyptians on the death of Apis. But all the women who refuse to let their hair be cut off, suffer the following punishment. On a fixed day they are obliged to prostitute themselves, and to this market only strangers are admitted, the proceeds being given to the temple of Aphrodite.'

This idea, of sexual activity as something which could be used as a punitive force, is alien to the rest of Greek life. The concept that the sexual instinct is a marvellous gift of nature or the gods, bringing one into mystical contact with the deity, which must be utilized and for which gratitude must be shown by a present to the goddess, sails dangerously if paradoxically near the reverse attitude in which it becomes a force requiring appeasement and sacrifice.

A very similar state of affairs was to be found among the Babylonians, in connexion with the worship of Mylitta, the Babylonian equivalent of Aphrodite. By a law of these people. every woman must, once in her life, go to the temple of Mylitta, and prostitute herself to the first stranger who presents himself. In the version of Herodotus: 'Many women, proud of their great wealth and desirous of keeping themselves apart from the vulgar, travel in a closed and covered carriage followed by a number of maidservants, into the temple . . . when a woman has once become seated she does not return home until one of the strangers has thrown a gold piece into her lap and had intercourse with her outside the temple; but, as he throws the money, he must at the same time say, "I demand you in the name of Mylitta." '

The hetairae were the friends of great men of every kind, soldiers, philosophers and artists. When Alexander the Great defeated Darius, he marched into Babylon, captured the city of Susa, and then entered Persepolis, the former capital. There was celebrated a spectacle in which a crowd of hetairae played a prominent and disastrous part, dominated and egged on by Thaïs, who had effected a liason, in spite of rumours of the contrariety of his interests, with Alexander himself. It was she who suggested the burning of the Persian palace, who led the drunken incendiarists, to the accompaniment of song, flute-playing and Bacchanalian dancing, and who threw the first torch.

The use of professional hetairae in religious festivals has already been mentioned. The Aphrodisia, although not officially recognized, were none the less popular for that, and were universally celebrated on Greek soil. They were, quite simply, festivals in honour of Aphrodite, and from them prostitutes and hetairae were seldom absent. A festival especially of the hetairae was the Aphrodisia of Aegina, where Phryne comported herself in the manner described by Athenaeus: 'But it was really Phryne who was more beautiful in her private parts, wherefore it was not easy to get a sight of her naked, for she wore round her body a tight-fitting chiton, and did not make use of the public baths. But at the festival of the Eleusinia and the Poseidonia, in the sight of all the Hellenes, she used to put off her himation, let down her hair, and go into the sea, and Apelles made her the model of his Aphrodite Anadyomene.'

The numerous prostitutes of Corinth celebrated the Aphrodisia in their own particularly lascivious and boisterous manner. The ceremony, known as a 'pannychis' (which became a favourite pet name for a hetaira), continued through-out the night. Although in theory a religious ceremony, it was in fact little more than a lecherous and bibacious rout. The 'foals of Aphrodite', 'almost naked in fine-spun clothes . . . sold their favours for a small fee which everyone might enjoy.'

The festival of Aphrodite Anosia, celebrated in Thessaly, was of a similar nature except that it was totally of a (female) homosexual character. Details are lacking, but erotic flagellation played an essential part.

Other festivals of a more or less national and definitely erotic character were the Dionysia (closely allied to the Roman worship of Liber, q.v.) and the Lenea, the feast of the wine-presses. This festival was marked by a great banquet, heavily subsidized by the state, and a dance through the city in fancy dress—Nymphs, Bacchantes, Satyrs, etc.—accompanied by wanton practical jokes of every kind, although primarily erotic. In March and April were celebrated the Elaphebolion, or City Dionysia. Choruses sang dithyrambs in honour of Dionysius, dances were performed by beautiful boys, in the evening people lay in the streets on couches drinking heavily. One or more phalli played a part in the entertainment.

In certain parts of Greece, in particular Cithaeron and Parnassus, and on the islands, a special Dionysia took place in which women and girls alone participated. At night, attired in Bacchic costume, goatskins, and with dishevelled hair, and carrying musical instruments, they climbed to the summit of an adjoining mountain and, stimulated to abnormal activity and excitement by the wine which they otherwise seldom if ever drank, they performed on the heights dances and sacrifices which rapidly achieved the category of orgies.

Pausanias, the Baedeker of ancient Greece, says apropos of Homer's speaking of 'the dancing-grounds of Panopeus', that he was much puzzled by this reference until it was explained to him 'by the women whom the Athenians call Thyiads'. 'These Thyiads are Attic women who go every year with the Delphian women to Parnassus, and there hold orgies in honour of Dionysius. It is the custom of these women to dance at various places on the road from Athens, and one of these places is Panopeus.' In another place, speaking of the Corycian cave, he says: 'The peaks are higher than the clouds, and the Thyiad women rave on them in honour of Dionysius and Apollo.'

The nature of these Dionysia must here be elaborated on, as they were different in an important respect from the kind of fertility festival familiar to everybody.

The Greek, when he was seized by some force compelling him to act in a manner different from that which he would normally have chosen, explained his sensations, naturally enough, as: 'possession by the gods'.

Unlike the Romans, this feeling inspired the Greeks with feelings of admiration rather than of obedience, but it did cause them to value everything which led to the achievement of a state of 'theolepsy'; of communion with the deity. This explains what to modern minds is at first difficult to comprehend, how the Greeks could regard indulgence in alcohol, dancing and copulation with sentiments of religious awe.

The purpose of the cult was therefore to facilitate an experience which the Greeks interpreted as a religiously ennobling one, although a modern psychologist would express their condition in very different terms, and although an objective perusal of the actions performed at these festivals leaves us with the impression of a sensual orgy.

None the less, the occasion was also used as a device for releasing sexual tension, and this is also true of fertility worship, even though this may have been regarded as a kind of spell to ensure, by an easy association of ideas, the success of the crops.

In the autumn the mysterious Eleusinian Mysteries were celebrated. The ceremony lasted nine days and its exact nature is difficult to determine. The idea behind it concerned the dying away and revivification of the grain. Vague notions of human immortality were also present.

The first days of the festival were occupied in processions to the sea, and ritual washings and purifications not always conducted with decorum and modesty. On the sixth day a procession left Athens for Eleusis. Those taking part, who were certainly numbered in thousands, were crowned with myrtle and ivy and carried lighted torches and ears of corn. Eleusis, nine miles distant, having been reached, the remainder of the period allotted to the celebrations was occupied in noisy, cheerful, and, although Titinios bluntly states that incest was a feature of the rites, esoteric activity.

Most of the ceremonies involving ceremonial copulation and other orgiastic behaviour, also involved a period of abstinence.

At the Attic Thesmophoria for example, one of the only truly national festivals, and known to us in part by the Thesmophoriazusae of Aristophanes: 'All the women who desired to take part in the festival were obliged to abstain from sexual intercourse for nine days before. The cleverness of the priests demanded this as an act of piety, the real reason of course being, that the women, whipped up by their long abstinence, might be able to take part in erotic orgies with less restraint. To strengthen themselves in this chastity that was demanded of them, which they probably found hard enough to preserve, women laid cooling herbs and leaves in their bed, especially Agnus Castus (λύγος ἄγνος — ἄγονος: making non-productive) and other plants (such as κνέωρον, κόνυζα). But according to Photius, at this time women ate garlic in order to frighten men away by the unappetizing smell of their mouth.'

However, it was in the worship and honour of Aphrodite that the most splendid, popular, and dissolute celebrations were performed. Aphrodite it was who gave to the Greeks and their gods the joys of love. Love and beauty were in the Greek mind inextricably intertwined and interdependent. Here above all others was matter for rejoicing and gratitude; for simple but enthusiastic expression of the emotions. Aphrodite is also the goddess of spring; of flowers; especially of the rose and myrtle with which she entwines herself as she walks through the woods. Animals follow her and fawn on her. Spring was the time when most of the Aphrodisia took place.

In Cyprus, an island thick with flowers, with fruit and with the perfume of innumerable blossoms, all the gifts of Aphrodite, at the place where the goddess had been born on the beach at Paphos, the most famous and luxurious of her ceremonies was begun. The image of the goddess was lovingly bathed in the sea, and decked with flowers, by girls who subsequently bathed themselves in preparation for the coming orgies of love, in cool streams running under groves of the sacred myrtle through valleys thick with almond blossom. The gods of the Greeks were the expression of their own feelings and emotions, glorified replicas of themselves and all that they would like to be. Unlike the Romans, who used their deities as scapegoats to whom forces they did not wish to acknowledge could be attributed, their worship was the worship of union, not of obedience. (Although Seleucus says it was not an ancient custom to indulge in wine or any other luxury to excess, except on the occasion of some sacred festival.) Statues of Aphrodite are those of a woman embodying in one form, every conceivable kind of feminine beauty. The Greeks always seem to have had a particular fondness for the human bottom, and so, with the delightful naïvety which could be found nowhere else, they set up temples and statues to Aphrodite Kallipygos, the goddess with the beautiful buttocks, and worshipped her with the grace mingled with uninhibited enthusiasm typical of the race. This, according to Athenaeus, arose from the following circumstances.

'A farmer had two beautiful daughters who once fell into a dispute with one another, and even went out on the highway to settle the question which of them had the more beautiful buttocks. One day a youth passed whose father was a rich old man, and to him they displayed themselves; and he, after gazing at them, decided in favour of the older girl; in fact he fell in love with her so passionately that when he returned to town he went to bed ill, and related what had happened to his brother, who was younger than he. So the latter also went into the country to gaze at the girls, and he too fell in love, but with the other girl. Now the father, at least, begged them to contract a more respectable marriage, but since he failed to persuade them, he brought the girls from their country home to his sons, having got the consent of the girls' father, and joined them in marriage to them. The girls, therefore, were called "the fair-buttocked" by the townspeople, as Cercidas of Megalopolis relates in his Iambic verses. He says: "there was a pair of fair-buttocked sisters in Syracuse". It was they, therefore, who, having come into the possession of splendid wealth, founded the temple of Aphrodite, calling the goddess "the Fair-Buttocked" as related also by Archelaus.'

A statue of Aphrodite Kallipygos can be seen in the Museo Nazionale at Naples. Erotic undoubtedly, but with a lack of any vulgarity not altogether attributable to the romance and reverence which tends to clog our assessment of objects in museums, the statue affords a momentary, partial, but revealing insight into the Greek attitude towards sex and life.

The Greek games were an expression of the delight of the people in the human body and its capabilities. It is very difficult for modern people, accustomed to the wearing of clothes, to understand the motives of the Greeks for nudity at the games, or to gauge the degree of eroticism present in their attitude towards them. That a sense of shame was occasioned by the wearing of clothes, not the reverse, and that garments were first assumed for climatic and hygienic reasons, is a theory now so generally accepted as to be a commonplace. The Greeks felt that to cover the private parts alone, when the rest of the body was unencumbered with clothing, would suggest some contempt, or feeling of shame for the genitals, when in fact their opinion on the subject was the exact opposite, the genitalia, as the instrument of exalted pleasure and miraculous fertility, inspiring them with gratitude and awe.

Eroticism, however, was only consciously, if at all, absent from these entertainments, and admiration of one kind of bodily function merged imperceptibly into another.

At Megara, the Diocleia games, in honour of the national

hero Diocles, were held in the spring; at these a kissing contest of beautiful boys was held which has been described by Theocritus. 'About his (i.e. Diocles') tomb, as soon as spring comes round, your children compete in a kissing-match, and he who most sweetly presses lip upon lip, returns laden with garlands to his mother.'

In Sparta, where the behaviour and outlook on life of the people was noticeably different from the rest of Greece, the Gymnopaedia, or naked boys' dance, was held annually as a kind of war memorial to the Spartans who had fallen at Thyrce. This was celebrated with dances and gymnastic performances by naked boys. The festival, so far from being regarded in the light of relaxation, was treated with such veneration as to be given preference over everything else.

The victor in the Olympic games, when he returned to his native city, was treated to profusions of honour and feasting. Covered in garlands he passed through the gates; songs were sung to him, statues in his image erected in the market place. He was treated for ever as an honoured citizen. His triumph was as great as that of any Roman general, and the superior percipience of the Greeks in this matter cannot be questioned by the unprejudiced.

Dances in connexion with various religious and local festivals occurred ubiquitously in Greece. Dancing in the form of the modern society dance was, of course, unknown. To them, dancing was a medium for the presentation in mime of internal ideas and emotions (and, as we have seen, for the achievement of a state of catharsis). Erotic dances, I mean for the moment those unconnected with religion, were in general use. Famous among these were the notorious Sicinnis and the Cordax. Both would be considered positively and primarily obscene by modern standards, involving as they did, suggestive movements and poses and the stripping off of all the clothes. The Satyrs in the Satyric dramas were presented as dancing the former and the quivering music of flutes accompanied them both.

Dancing by both male guests and female 'cup-bearers' was

a usual feature of banquets. Lasciviousness as such might be applauded, but lack of elegance and self-control was condemned and despised.

Cleisthenes, the ruler of Sicyon, had a daughter, Agariste, whose beauty was so great that suitors had filled his house for more than a year, and he used the opportunity to test them thoroughly. Hippocleides, at the end of the scrutiny appeared the best of the bunch, and on the final day a banquet was held at which the suitors displayed their social and musical aptitudes. Hippocleides, who had drunk rather too much, performed a suggestive dance to the music of flutes, finally getting carried away so far as to stand on his head on the table and wave his legs about in the air. His would-be father-in-law, who by now had lost his temper and his patience, told him that he had danced away his bride. The unrepentant performer replied 'Hippocleides cares not' and left the hall laughing.

Restraint and dignity were most important personal attainments in Greek eyes. The cup-bearers at banquets were practically invariably boys. The method of presenting the cup was considered a great art—which according to Xenophon was best understood by the Persians. Lucian tells an interesting story in this connexion.

'I had seen a beautiful young slave who was appointed to act as cup-bearer, and stood behind Cleodemus smiling, and I was interested to know the reason. I therefore watched him closely, and as the beautiful Ganymede soon drew near again to take back the drinking cup from Cleodemus, I noticed that the latter stroked his finger, and, as it seemed to me, together with the cup pressed a couple of drachmae into his hand. The boy smiled again at his finger being stroked, but I thought he did not notice the money. Consequently the two drachmae fell rattling on the floor, at which the philosopher and the boy became very red.'

Cleodemus denied all knowledge of the money, and so did the boy, but the master of the house took occasion to have the cup-bearer removed. Cleodemus' disgrace lay in two things.

His inability as a *philosopher* to control his emotions, and his having anything whatever to do with a slave.

Although women were probably never used as cup-bearers, girls in the form of slaves and hetairae were undoubtedly present, and these might, as a joke, once intoxication had reached a certain point, be induced to pour out the wine. As a permanent job this remained the privilege and duty of the young slaves.

These dancing-girls and flute players were expected to serve multiple purposes, for besides satisfying, to one extent or another, the sexual requirements of the banqueters, they were also supposed to fulfil the other functions of entertainment suggested by their names.

The people of Colophon (mentioned above) says Phylarchus; 'passed a law, which was still in force in our day, that the flute-girls and harp-girls and all such entertainers should receive wages from early in the morning until midday, and from then until lamplight . . .' And Theopompus claims of the Thessalians that: 'their lives are spent in the case of some of them in the continual company of dancing-girls and flute-girls, while others pass the livelong day in gaming, drinking, and the like forms of dissipation. . . .'

The Cardians, perhaps by way of variety, 'had schooled their horses to dance at their drinking-parties to the accompaniment of the pipes, and rising on their hind legs, and, as it were, gesticulating with their front feet, they would dance, being thoroughly accustomed to the pipe melodies.' This peculiar practice was to be turned against them, for their enemies sought out and purchased a Cardian flute-girl, who taught many musicians the tunes to which the animals were accustomed to dance, so that when battle was joined, the Cardian cavalry was suddenly disrupted by the playing of the familiar music.

The fear that luxury might undermine military strength and security seems to have been the principal argument brought forward in its disfavour, and with certain good reason.

Polycrates, the Tyrant of Samos, was overthrown by his preoccupation with pleasure—or according to Clearchus, 'Polycrates, the tyrant of Samos, came to ruin on account of his dissipated mode of life, emulating as he did the effeminate practices of the Lydians. From this motive he constructed in the city the famous "quarter" of Samos, to rival the park at Sardis called "Sweet Embrace": and in competition with the flowers (i.e. products connected with luxury) of Lydia he wove the widely heralded flowers of the Samians. Of these two innovations, the Samian Quarter was a lane crowded with professional women, and he literally filled Hellas with all kinds of food that tempted to sensuality and incontinence. The flowers of the Samians, on the other hand, are the various charms of men and women. But while the whole city was still engaged in holiday revels and drunken orgies, the Persians attacked and conquered it.' The Lacedaemonians prudently kept an eye on the physique of their army, compelling the soldiery to parade naked once a week, to check pot-bellies and other results of physical indulgence. A weekly inspection of bedding was also conducted to make sure that a too-soft mattress was not undermining the morale of the troops.

The generalizations of Athenaeus or his sources concerning entire nations are less valuable than the portraits of individuals. Some of these, concerning Dionysius of Sicily and Sardanapalus have already been quoted. Of the latter ruler a further story is told by Ctesias. Arbaces, a Mede, desired an interview with Sardanapalus, and by intrigue obtained one. 'When the Mede entered, he saw the king with his face covered with white lead, and bejewelled like a woman, combing purple wool in the company of his concubines, and sitting among them with knees uplifted, his eyebrows blackened, wearing a woman's dress and having his beard shaved close and his face rubbed with pumice (he was even whiter than milk and his eyelids were painted) and when he looked upon Arbaces he rolled the whites of his eyes.' Varying accounts of the death of this king are given. According to some, Arbaces, overcome by fury and disgust to think that such a person should be his king, stabbed Sardanapalus there and then. But in other versions he died in his bed; and in another he perished in an enormous and elaborate suicidal funeral pyre in company with his concubines, his queen, his treasure, and his entire wardrobe. The pyre burnt for fifteen days, exciting much speculation and comment but no interference. The Greeks were extremely well aware of the androgynous nature of human beings, and one finds surprisingly often accounts of men of otherwise virile habits and apparent heterosexual preferences appearing in public in women's clothes. This custom played a part in festivals as well as in the lives of individuals. At the Oscophoria, celebrated in the month of Pyanepsion (November-December) and named after the Oschoi or branches of vine with grapes on them, the branches were carried by two beautiful boys dressed as girls. At Amathus in Cyprus a male-female divinity was worshipped, a part of which ceremony was performed by a youth who lay in simulated child-bed imitating the cries of a woman in labour. This took place in honour of Ariadne, who landed on the island with Theseus and died there in childbirth.

Another figure addicted to this dressing-up was Androcottus, a Phrygian, and Sagaris the Mariandynian. The latter 'in his luxurious indulgence was until he was an old man fed at the lips of his nurse, not wishing to take the trouble to chew, and . . . he never carried his hand down lower than his navel. Wherefore Aristotle used to say jokingly of Xenocrates of Chalcedon that when he made water he never put his hand to his member, and he would quote "my hands are pure, it is my mind that has a taint!" '

The same awareness of the bi-sexuality of man appears in the flagellation common at erotic festivals, which, unlike that of the Romans, was untinged with guilt. It is not really surprising that transvestism should so frequently be a feature of these festivals. Human beings may or may not be aware of their bi-sexuality. In the course of everyday life it is necessary to suppress these inclinations.

Theopompus, author of the *History of King Philip*, says that Straton, King of Sidon, 'overtopped all men in pleasure and luxury. . . . Straton . . . used to arrange his parties in the company of flute-girls, singing-girls, and girls who played on the harp; and he used to summon many courtesans from Peloponnessus, many singing-girls from Ionia, besides girls from every part of Greece, some of whom were singers, some dancers; he was in the habit of getting up contests among them in the company of his friends, and in their society he spent all his time, since he himself enjoyed this kind of life, being by nature a slave to his pleasures, but still more because he strove to outdo Nicocles.' (A novel and interesting angle on debauchery this; the snob motive.) 'For, as it happens they were exceedingly jealous of each other, and each was eager to live in greater pleasure and ease than the other. . . .'

Theopompus goes on to mention another lover of luxury, Cotys, King of Thrace. This king, whenever in his wanderings about the country he came upon a situation which took his fancy, would have it converted into an alfresco banqueting place, and these he visited in turn. This Cotys got up a magnificent banquet on the whimsical pretext that Athena was to be married to him . . . 'and after erecting a bridal chamber he awaited the goddess in a drunken revel. And presently going entirely out of his senses, he dispatched one of his bodyguard to see whether the goddess had arrived at the bridal chamber. When the poor fellow returned with the announcement that there was nobody in the chamber, Cotys shot him dead with his bow, and then killed a second messenger for the same reason: until the third man sagaciously said that the goddess had arrived a long while before and was waiting for him. This king once, in a fit of jealousy against his own wife, cut up the poor woman with his own hand beginning with the pudenda.'

Chares, the Athenian general, used to cart about with him on his campaigns flute-girls, harp-girls, and prostitutes and used to devote a portion of the money subscribed for the war to maintaining these comforts, sending some of it back to Athens for the enjoyment of private individuals and the use of financially embarrassed persons against whom lawsuits were pending. This naturally made him extremely popular among the citizens, 'for they themselves lived in that (i.e. one similar to Chares') manner, so that the young men spent all their time among paltry little flute-girls and in the houses of prostitutes, while those who were a little older than they indulged in drinking-bouts and gambling, and the like prodigalities; and the populace as a whole squandered more money on the public banquets and distributions of meat than on the administration of the state.' So Theopompus.

Heracleides of Pontus, in his work 'On Pleasure', says of Themistocles that 'when as yet the Athenians were not addicted to carousing or resorting to prostitutes, (he) openly yoked four courtesans to a chariot and drove them through the Ceramicus when it was crowded.' This story is slightly spoiled by Idomeneus who, in his account, leaves it open to doubt whether the hetairae were actually drawing, or merely seated in, the chariot containing Themistocles. However, a similar story is told of Mark Anthony.

The Greeks, as might be expected, put even the conduct of a military campaign second to the pleasure which made life and liberty worth keeping, and in enlightened contrast to modern politicians, sacrificed military power to maintain a standard of comfort which would remind the citizens at home what it was that they were fighting to defend. Alexander the Great, himself no passive belligerent, was much addicted to luxury.

During dinner he liked to be entertained by the performances of every kind of contestant, dancer and musician. The general himself liked to take part, and on these occasions, he pledged his toasts, contrary to the custom of the times, in unmixed wine, compelling others to do likewise. At banquets he would appear attired in a varied sequence of costumes,

masquerading as deities both male and female, wearing sometimes the horns of the ram-headed Egyptian god, and sometimes the dress of Artemis. On other occasions, according to his
mood, 'he bore the lion's skin and club in imitation of Heracles.'
'At still other times he was garbed in the costume of Hermes . . .
as a rule, and in everyday use, he wore a purple riding-cloak,
a purple tunic with white stripes, and the Macedonian hat with
the royal fillet. At Ectabana he arranged a festival in honour
of Dionysius, everything being supplied at the feast with lavish
expense, and Satrabates the Satrap entertained all the troops.'

According to Chares (the historian, not the general),
Alexander, 'when he overcame Darius . . . concluded marriages
of himself and of his friends besides, constructing ninety-two
bridal chambers in the same place. The structure was large
enough for a hundred couches, and in it every couch was
adorned with nuptial coverings, and was made of silver worth
twenty minae, but his own couch had supports of gold. He
also included in his invitation to the banquet all his personal
friends, and placed them on couches opposite himself and the
other bridegrooms. . . . The structure was decorated sumptu-
ously and magnificently with expensive draperies and fine
linens, and underfoot with purple and crimson rugs interwoven
with gold. To keep the pavillion firmly in place there were
columns thirty feet high, gilded and silvered and studded with
jewels. The nuptials lasted five days and very many persons
contributed their services.'

Alexander, says Polycleitus of Larisa, was always accompanied to camp by flute-players, both male and female, who
drank with him until daybreak.

A wedding was and is an unfailing excuse for a banquet,
and many such must have been held; one stands out above the
others in magnificence—the celebrations in connexion with
the marriage of Caranus, in Macedonia. This has been described at length by Athenaeus, and in fact, judging by the
quantity of food and number of entertainments listed, must
have continued over a considerable period of time. It was really

not one feast but a continuous series: for bouts of eating alternated with bouts of amusement. There were twenty guests,
who, in the course of the evening, managed to collect from their
generous host a great many presents, mostly in the form of
plates and goblets of flamboyantly expensive design, and after a
preliminary *hors d'oeuvres* of gigantic size, consisting of chickens,
ducks, ringdoves, geese, hares, young goats, 'curiously moulded
cakes', pigeons, turtle-doves, partridges and 'other fowl in
plenty' and when, in the description of Hippolochus 'we had
at last pleasantly taken leave of all sobriety, there entered
flute-girls and singers, and some Rhodian sambuca-players.
To me these girls looked quite naked, but some said they had
on tunics.' (These would have been the famous Coan garments.
The manufacturers of Cos learnt to achieve a cobweb fineness
in their products, which were denounced by the more conserva-
tive, and eagerly purchased by the go-ahead and fashionable.
Many were exported to Rome.)

These entertainers were followed by a large pig, which
entered 'on a silver platter gilded all over to no little thickness.'
The pig 'lay on its back . . . the belly, seen from above, dis-
closed that it was full of many bounties. For, roasted inside it
were thrushes, ducks, and warblers in unlimited quantities,
pease purée poured over eggs, oysters and scallops. . . .'

More amusement followed this staggering blow-out, which
must have provided a substantial helping for each of the
twenty guests. Dancers, clowns, and some naked female
jugglers now appeared 'who performed tumbling acts among
swords, and blew fire from their mouths.'

Food and performances alternated again, a drinking bout
following the naked female jugglers. 'Our attention was engros-
sed in a warm and almost neat drink, the wines at our disposal
being Thasian, Mendaean and Lesbian; and very large gold
cups handed to each guest.' Baked fish and presents of crystal
plates followed this selection which was in turn succeeded by
more dancing-girls dressed as Nereids and Nymphs and a
splendid living tableau of Cupids and Dianas, Pans and

Hermae, who held torches in silver brackets. The guests, who were apparently still standing, for: 'the wonderful thing about it was that, although relaxed and heavy with wine, as soon as we saw any of these things introduced we all became sober enough to stand on our feet', were only expected to endure one more course, for after being served with boars skewered with silver spears and laden with presents they were allowed to reel home 'quite sober . . . the gods be our witness! . . . because we were apprehensive for the safety of the wealth we took with us.'

Altogether rather too much food, and possibly a too gastronomic orgy to qualify unreservedly; but weddings stimulate erotic thoughts in the minds of the guests, and although the sexual nature of a social function should be appreciable objectively rather than subjectively if it is to be accurately described as an orgy, the outlet, although vicarious, is unquestionable, and I feel that a point should be stretched and the qualification allowed.

Alexander was by all accounts very much addicted to drink, but extreme alcoholism was rare in Ancient Greece, although Dionysius of Sicily is reputed to have permanently injured his eyesight through this form of excess, having once been sozzled for ninety consecutive days, and Nysaeus, who became tyrant of Syracuse, drank and stuffed himself with food 'as though he had been apprehended on a capital charge, and saw that he had only a few months more to live.' This ruler, when intoxicated, became exceedingly lecherous and took to the outraging of both boys and women. The Sicilians appear to have had a reputation for an unusual degree of indulgence in food and drink. Plato was unfavourably impressed by this habit, and remarked: 'The life there satisfied me in no way or manner; think of a life of stuffing twice a day, and never being able to lie alone at night, to say nothing of all the other practices which accompany that mode of living.' Diotimus of Athens earned himself the nickname of 'funnel' for 'he would insert a funnel in his mouth and drink unceasingly while the wine poured in.'

Orgies of rape inflicted by a conquering army on the defeated civilians are more in keeping with the ex-Hellenic world than with the nature of the Greek people. The Scythians, however, living on the boundaries of Greece, once they 'had tasted the sweet fruit of luxury proceeded' according to the account of Clearchus 'so far in insolence that they cut off the noses of all men into whose lands they penetrated . . . and their women tattooed the bodies of the women in the Thracian tribes who lived near them on the west and north, injecting the design with pins.'

All the same, compare the story of Dionysius and the girls of Locris (above). These were subjects, not a conquered people, but Dionysius was an individual, not a 'conformist' and, moreover, an individual who excited the very material displeasure of contemporary morality.

Why, one asks oneself, did the Greeks need the orgy system, since their outlook was so healthy, so Hedonistic? Why did they not let the tension, sexual and otherwise, ooze out little by little in the course of everyday life. The answer is something of an imponderable. It is easy to exaggerate the Hedonism of the Greeks, and many have done so. What should be remembered is the outstanding balance of Greek life, that they did not allow their pursuit of one thing to destroy their enjoyment of another. Marriage might afford opportunities for sensual delight, it also had other aspects such as the procreation and proper education of children. In the *Odyssey*, Nestor calls to Athene: 'But O' Queen, be propitious and grant me fair renown, to me myself and to my children, and to my revered wife.' The Greeks saw that unbounded sexual indulgence would lead to the sexual satisfaction of nobody, and that it might destroy other things worth having by the way. (Even the cathartic festivals such as the Dionysia were held at infrequent though regular intervals.) For all their naïvety the Greeks were eminently practical people, they were realists enough to know that the inclination was there and to save the whole boiler they loosened the safety-valve from time to time.

Moreover, they knew that Hedonism is not always identical with the gratification of the moment. None the less, the trace of the old Victorian idea is present—women are either whores or mothers, they cannot combine the two. The heart of the matter lies in the fact already mentioned, the fact that lies behind the orgy as a phenomenon of society, that men are part human, part animal, and that the interests of the two conflict. The wife becomes inacceptable as a bedfellow *because* she is the wife, and because she is also the person who is fulfilling the functions of housewife and mother.

One of the results of the seclusion of women was the prevalence of homosexuality—a similar state of affairs to that found in Moslem countries.

This was an alternative safety-valve. It was not blocked, but in the hands of the Greeks it became, like most things they touched, idealized.

As a result of this idealization, there grew up a relationship the exact nature of which is very hard to judge.

Love between an older man and a younger, thought desirable because of the influence that such a relationship would have on the general behaviour of the younger man. It was thought, probably correctly, that a desire to be thought admirable would affect the behaviour and achievement of the youth in every way. The point at which the relationship merged from the sentimental to the physical is problematical, as are the reasons for which the Greeks decided not to seal this outlet, but to glorify it.

The Greeks, as has already been stated, have been dealt with at some length, because they are one of the two civilized societies who last included the orgy as a part of the national outlook, as an officially recognized way of blowing-off steam. This did not mean, as we have seen, that there were not also 'rebel' orgiasts in Greek society and this is interesting and significant, though of what it is too early to say. The Romans, who are dealt with next, are the others. Unfortunately, the usefulness of the orgy is coupled with the danger of its deterioration. One of these two peoples, who provided two patterns, with one or other of which the rebel orgiasts of subsequent generations can be classed, was in my opinion infinitely more wholesome, successful, and clear-minded about the true purpose of the orgy and, in a curious way, the whole nature of sexuality than the other. The argument must not be anticipated—the successors of the Greeks will now be examined and the comparisons should make themselves.

TWO

THE ROMANS

No greater difference can be imagined than that which existed between the philosophy of life of the Romans and that of the Greeks, judged by the knowledge that we have of the ordinary people of the two civilizations.

In his everyday life the Greek, as we have seen, displayed an unmistakable zest for life which was accompanied by grace, style and understanding in and for the art of living: in the eating of his food, the wearing of his clothes and in the control of his sexuality. One of the first impressions that one receives in reading about this aspect of the lives of the two peoples is that the Greeks controlled their sexuality, but that the sexuality of the Romans became their master, that they abandoned themselves to this master, and that he destroyed them as they had foreseen and partially intended.

Greek sexual life was extraordinarily free from perversions. (I exclude homosexuality from this category, since it does not arise from a mistaken concept of sexuality.) One of the surest signs of the presence or absence of disease in the sexual life of a civilization is to be found in its literature, and by this standard the Romans stand condemned, just as the Greeks pass the test as well as, if not better than, any modern nation. This, like any other ethical judgement is essentially subjective not objective, but much of the *un*happiness resulting from sexuality appears to me to be only caused by a partial and possibly unconscious renunciation of sexual activity, therefore I do not think that sexuality can justifiably be regarded in any measure a possible cause of misery but rather as a cause of happiness.

43

The literature of the Greeks contains many references to homosexual love, but, as we have seen, this love is always idealized, admired and mystified: the whole Greek attitude indicated an appreciation of and admiration for the possibilities of purely sensual delights, undefiled by the heresy that it is impossible to mix intellectual and physical pleasures, which leads inevitably and undesirably to the sacrifice of one to the other.

When we look at the literature of the Romans we see something different. It is not as obvious as one might expect, but it is there, nevertheless, an obsession with cruelty, more important, an *attitude towards* cruelty, which is to be seen nowhere in the literature of the Hellenics. That this presence was reflected in actual life, everyone is aware. I am fairly convinced in my own mind as to the cause of this phenomenon, and if I am right, this cause is exceedingly relevant to an examination of the ways in which the Romans sought their pleasures, and why, as I shall try to show, they failed. First, I want to demonstrate the quite amazing extent to which the thanatic instincts came to make themselves felt in the life of the people.

The Greeks, of course, like everybody else, had feelings of aggressiveness and sadistic desires, but the word 'sadism' is in fact here singularly inappropriate, for the whole essence of the Greek attitude towards these instincts was its complete freedom from morbidity. Orgiastic festivals such as the Dionysia served not only as a means of achieving the 'theolepsy' already described, but also served, as I have said, as a safety-valve to thanatic as well as erotic instincts.

This latter (the safety-valve) is the true function of the orgy, the notion of theolepsy being a romanticized explanation by semi-primitive man of things which he did not lucidly comprehend.

Many people will not admit to their sadistic instincts, others become completely fascinated by them. In this fact lies one of the dangers of the orgy if it is used by people who do not understand its nature. The Romans were such a people.

There are those who find it incredible that individuals derive actual pleasure, pleasure of an erotic origin, from the contemplation of suffering. That there are, or at any rate were, people who derive pleasure from contemplating actual death, with or without torture, is more incredible but unfortunately still less capable of being rejected on the grounds of subjective incomprehensibility.

According to Rosenbaum large numbers of prostitutes (*History of Syphilis*) used to assemble in brothels near the Circus Maximus, for the purpose of intercepting as they returned from the games, men who had been raised to a high pitch of sexual excitement by the gladiatorial shows, the mutilations by and of wild animals, and all the other obsessional insanities of the arena. One of the most prominent, repellent and characteristic features of these ceremonies was the organization, the high degree of ritual with which they were performed. It is this, the elaboration, the planning, the constant devising of new implements of torture, the odious ceremony, which brands the Romans as perverts. Into every newly invented mode of execution, into every torture was always brought one feature, the flogging of the victim or of the condemned man. It was not enough to be killed. Death was nothing, a mere negation, there must be positive pain first. 'Strike so that he feels he is dying,' said Caligula, and although it may be thought unfair to quote the words of an epileptic and a lunatic, history shows with hideous but fascinating clarity that in his time Caligula's outlook was not confined to one man, or even to a small circle. Everywhere we look we find the same thing. Roman society was based on slaves and these slaves were treated abominably, not only by their masters but by their mistresses as well; nor can this cruelty be explained away on the grounds of necessity, the different humanitarian conventions of past ages, or by anything else other than the simple and interesting truth. Juvenal attacks the sadism of women.

45

But you should know what Everywoman does
at home all day. Suppose her husband turns
his back to her in bed. God help the housemaid!
The lady's maids are stripped, the coachman's thrashed
for being late (punished because another slept)
rods are broken, bleeding backs are scourged
and lashed: some women keep a private flogger.
She scourges while her face is made up, talks
to her friends, examines a gold-braided frock
and thrashes, reads the daily paper through
and thrashes, til the thrasher tires, and she
screams GO NOW, and the inquisition's over.
She rules her home more savagely than a tyrant.
Has she an assignation, wants to look
more beautiful than usual, quick, he's waiting
under the trees, or in Queen Isis' brothel,
poor Psecas combs the mistress's hair, her own
tattered, with naked shoulders and bare breasts
"This curl's too high." At once the oxhide thong
lashes the wretch, her crime was a coiffure.

Juvenal's account is not without its sexual undertones.

In seeking the cause of a feature so prominent in a society, one naturally examines the system of education. Here, as elsewhere, we find the same old story, the frequent and severe floggings, the indoctrination in aggressive manhood which, as in the situation which was to echo it two thousand years later, could only lead to eventual misery for all concerned. But it is to be questioned whether these elements in Roman and German education should be accepted as causes or whether they are not rather a mere result, a symptom of the original disease.

The cruelty of the games, and the luxuriance of private individuals increased as military activity declined. For many years the Romans had indulged in cruelty and violence more or less incidental to their ultimate aims. When the need ceased, they found that none the less they could not break themselves of the habit. What had started as something non-sexual had become by stealth based in eroticism. This is a process which can be, and has been, observed elsewhere, particularly in the case of religious cults. The sexual instinct is very strong, the capacities of the human mind for creating sexual symbolism unlimited. Small wonder then if eroticism is so pervasive. Every human being is to some extent polymorphically perverse, the seeds of many perversions lie in all of us, and of these seeds none responds so easily to fertilization as those of sadism and masochism. The sadism of the games undoubtedly aroused an echo in the hearts of many. Augustine tells the following story:

'A young Christian was living in Rome as a student. He had long avoided the amphitheatre, but was at last taken to visit it by friends. He told them that they could drag his body there but not his soul, for he would sit with his eyes closed, and so be really absent. This he did, but a great shout induced him to open his eyes in curiosity. Then his soul was stricken more sorely than the bodies of those he yearned to see, and his fall was more lamentable than that which had caused the shout. For with the sight of blood he absorbed a lust for cruelty; he could not turn away; his gaze grew fixed; he was drunk with the lust for blood. Why should I say more? He looked, his blood burned, and he took away with him a madness which goaded him to return again.'

Behind the sado-masochistic idea lies an equation of violence and copulation. This implies various preliminary ideas. First that in sex there exists something foul and criminal, second, following on from this, that the active participants are committing an offence on the passive. Following this will come the impulse-desire towards retribution.

The possessor of either of these perversions has, at some level of his consciousness, gone astray. Either he has, by a tortuous and mistaken process of subconscious thinking, decided that he must sacrifice his sexuality to save his conscience and the people with whom he comes in contact. Or, in the case of the sadist, he will be tortured by a well-founded guilt.

47

This is what I believe happened in the case of Imperial Rome. Because the Romans behaved brutally it does not follow, and indeed would be the greatest possible error to conclude, that they were basically and entirely brutal men. Nobody is an entirely straightforward character, nobody is entirely free from animal instincts, but nobody is completely an animal, and nobody who is not an animal can be completely free from conscience.

Roman society was balanced on a society of slaves. It was built on a debt which the slave-masters owed to the slaves, which they might pretend not to recognize, which they might attempt to adjust within themselves, but which would be a potential and constant danger to their peace of mind.

This is not fanciful Freudian speculation. An examination of the pleasures of the Romans will reveal many of the characteristics of the obsessional gambler, who acts ostensibly in the hopes of winning, but whose behaviour indicates that he is also attracted by the notion that he may lose, and who extracts his pleasure largely from this element of danger to himself. This characteristic appears again and again in Roman activities. The Romans were not Hedonists, no matter how passionately they were addicted to luxury, because it must have been obvious to them, as to their posterity, that what they were doing contained an element of the suicidal, and was bound to defeat its own ends. The Hedonist is not necessarily betraying his philosophy by buying present happiness at the price of future misery, unless in the back of his mind he uses 'buy' as we say of a criminal released from jail that he has 'paid' for what he has done. Too often this confusion is made.

So far the picture painted is gloomy enough, it is an accurate representation, but not all the Romans were practising sadists. Apart from the individual exceptions to any rule, there were plenty of aspects of Roman life where the dominating preoccupation of the race lay quiescent, although strangely enough it is some of these which have received the brunt of the abuse showered on the 'decadent' Roman state.

Sado-masochism represents one misconception of the nature of sexuality, religion represents another, as we have seen in the case of the Greeks. Perhaps this is not quite accurate. Sadism represents a misconception, religion an idealization. Both are inferior to an acceptance of sex at its face value, but the latter is infinitely preferable to the former. One represents defeat, the other a compromise. One can cause infinite harm, the other little.

Nearly all the Roman deities connected with sexual life, whether imported or indigenous, rapidly became discoloured by the character of their human progenitors.

Venus, theoretically the goddess of love, appears in Roman life in several different, almost irreconcilable forms. She was the guardian of honourable marriage, her worship being celebrated by the *matronae*, the mothers of families. But this impression of her character, as being essentially unconnected with pure lust, is set at naught by the discovery that she was also the patron of *meretrices*—of harlots. Thirdly, and possibly most significantly, she was in some way the mother of the Roman nation. (In view of the fact that the symbol of the Roman state was the *fasces*, this connexion between the nation and the erotic instinct is, to say the least, interesting.) Confusing us still further, *Venus* appears a fourth time as *Venus Verticordia*, the turner of hearts (from licentiousness). The worship of this form of the deity originated in 114 B.C. when three Vestal Virgins were condemned to death for disobeying the laws against sexual intercourse. It is difficult to make much of this confusing goddess, whose different forms were all celebrated at different festivals. The patroness of harlots, called *Volgivaga*, or street-walker, had her festival on 23 April, according to Ovid, who, unfortunately, does not particularize. The whole worship of *Venus* shows the capacity of the Ancients for transforming into the form of cults, many subjects which to modern minds are quite unsuited to deification.

The worship of a deity known as *Fortuna Virilis*, said by some to be connected with *Venus*, and worshipped by women

of the poorer classes in the *men's* baths, and the naïve explanation that 'there, those parts of the male body are uncovered
which seek women's favour' display the same rather Hellenic
attitude.

The god *Liber*, at any rate in his origin, was a comparatively
straightforward fertility god. In various parts of Italy he was
honoured by Phallic cults. In these a large wooden phallus
was ceremoniously carried on a cart through the city and fields,
finally being crowned by a matron. The Romans may or may
not have originally conceived him as being unconnected with
any fertility other than that of the soil, the symbolism was
obvious and convenient, and another element soon began to
creep in. Augustine refers to these ceremonies:

'Varro says among other things that the rites of *Liber* were
celebrated at the crossroads in Italy so immodestly and
licentiously that the male genitals were worshipped in honour
of the god . . . and this not with any modest secrecy but with
open and exulting depravity. That shameful part of the body
was, during the festival of *Liber*, placed with great pomp on
wagons and carried about to the crossroads in the country,
and at last into the city. In the town of Lanuvium, a whole
month was dedicated to *Liber*. During it all the citizens used
the most disgraceful words until the phallus had been carried
across the market place and put to rest again. It was necessary
that the most honourable of the matrons should publicly place a
wreath on that disgraceful effigy. The god *Liber* had to be
propitiated to ensure the future of the crops, and the evil eye
had to be repelled from the fields by compelling a married
woman to do in public, that which not even a harlot might
do under the eyes of married women in a theatre.'

Kiefer says that 'the fact that the ceremony was performed
by an honourable woman shows that it was not a piece of
debauchery, but an old custom of religious significance to
avert destructive magical influences.' There is a little, but not
much, in what he says. An examination of result is more often
than not a reliable means of judging cause. If people behave in

a partly or totally erotic manner, it is surely not uncharitable to assume that their motive is, in its absolute origin, partly or wholly sexual. In cases where an intellectual process is given as the motive for sexual behaviour the reverse is more likely to be the case.

Kiefer goes on to deal with the phallus as an amulet against the evil eye, attempting to isolate the emblem in this form from its erotic one.

'A phallus was sometimes set up above city gates as a protection against ill-luck. Sometimes under such a phallus appears the inscription *"Hic Habitat Felicitas"*—happiness dwells here. This, of course, does not mean that the place guaranteed any sort of sexual happiness, only that the phallus expelled unhappiness by its magic.'

But the idea that Kiefer so airily dismisses is not wholly ridiculous. The phallus *is* capable of bringing to both men and women happiness of one sort at any rate, and the nature of this gift being in truth miraculous appeared to semi-civilized man to be of a magical nature.

Kiefer goes on to mention the number of phallic amulets in the possession of museums, which are hidden away from the gaze of the general public. 'The man of today views these things almost with the eyes of St. Augustine, and so, does no justice to the deep original meaning of the symbol.'

One cannot help receiving the impression that the man of today in his naïveté, and St. Augustine, apart from his moral judgements, are right, and that Kiefer, in his sophistication, is wrong. The meaning which he describes as 'original', is in truth only a development of the true original, which must have been, even if not consciously so, erotic.

Priapus, the garden god, is still more openly phallic. In theory a mere scarecrow, like *Liber*, his erotic element came to dominate his cult. Sometimes his entire figure was in the form of an immense phallus, into which a human head and features had been incorporated. Nearly always he was equipped with a genital organ of stupendous size. At any rate, whether the god had or had not original sexual associations, the imagination of the people soon transformed him into a totally sexual deity, and the characteristics of his sexuality were those of his worshippers. The phallus of *Priapus* is frequently conceived as a weapon, or instrument of punishment, as the well-known collection of Latin poems known as the '*Priapeia*' show. A strongly sadistic tone runs through all these poems, and in the festivals connected with the Priapic cult a similar element is to be found. Petronius has parodied such a festival in the *Satyricon* when he described the defloration of Pannychis, a little girl of seven by Giton, a boy hardly older, and described before this ceremony as 'of the most retining'.

The cult of the *Bacchanalia* originated in Southern Italy and spread northwards with irresistible force. An unusually high element of hysteria, violence and sexual activity was associated with these festivals, and they did not meet with official approval. At first they were more or less tolerated, as the words of Livy show.

'You know well senators, that the *Bacchanalia*, which have long been widespread in Italy, are now flourishing in Rome: you know this not only by hearsay, but by the noises and shrieks which resound through the city at night.'

That the *Bacchanalia* came to be regarded with disfavour by the majority of citizens, we know from a story recounted by Livy in which the hysteria and self-destructive abandon which were an essential part of the ceremony become apparent.

A young man called Aebutius had formed a liaison with a freedwoman named Hispala, who had once been a notorious whore. His mother and stepfather wished, for financial reasons, to destroy him, and this they determined to do by inducing him to take part in the *Bacchanalia*. The mother called the boy and told him that while he was ill she had sworn an oath to initiate him into the Bacchic rites. He must therefore abstain from sexual intercourse for ten days in preparation for the ceremony of initiation. On the last day, after supper, when he had bathed and purified himself; she would take him to the shrine.

When Hispala learned of the mother's intention, or guessed it when Aebutius warned her that he would be spending several nights away from her, she was appalled, saying that it would be better for them both to be dead rather than that he should do anything so foolish. Questioned further she said that while she was still a slave she had accompanied her mistress to the shrine, which she knew to be the abode of 'all kinds of corruption. It was known she said, that for two years no one older than twenty had been initiated. Whenever a man was introduced he was handed over to the priests like a beast for the slaughter. They took him to a place which resounded with cries, hymns and the beating of drums and cymbals . . . so that no one could hear the victim's cries for help while he was being violated.'

On his return home, Aebutius revealed to his mother and stepfather his intention of having nothing whatever to do with the *Bacchanalia*, and they in a fury drove him from the house. On the advice of his aunt he went before the consul Postumius and told his story. The consul, having assured himself of the reliability of the young man, sent for, and interrogated the woman Hispala. At first terror made her deny everything, but finally she told her story.

'She said that the shrine had at first been reserved for women, and that no men had been admitted. There had been three special days every year on which initiations took place. Married women had taken it in turns to be priestesses. Then a Campanian woman had changed the whole ritual, ostensibly at the command of the gods. She had begun by initiating two men, her sons. After the rites had become open to everybody, so that men attended as well as women, and their licentiousness increased with the darkness of night, there was no shameful or criminal deed from which they shrank. The men were guilty of more immoral acts among themselves than the women. Those who struggled against dishonour or were slow to inflict it on others, were slaughtered in sacrifice like brute beasts. The holiest article of their faith was to think nothing a crime. The men prophesied like madmen with their bodies distorted by frenzy. The women dressed as Bacchantes with their hair unbound, ran down to the Tiber carrying burning torches which they plunged into the water and brought out still burning, because they had been smeared with sulphur and lime. They said "the gods have taken them" when certain men were bound to a windlass and snatched away out of sight into secret caverns. Those were the men who had refused either to take the oath, or to join in the crimes, or to be violated. The society had a huge membership, almost half (*sic*) the population ... and among them were men and women of noble birth.'

As a result of this statement the consul obtained the consent of the horrified senate to conduct a full investigation. Finally he made his report to the senate, in which, according to Livy, he said: 'A great number of adherents are women, which is the origin of the whole trouble. But there are also men like women, who have joined in each other's defilement, fanatics maddened by night-watching, by wine, by nightly shrieking and uproar. ... If you knew the age at which the men are initiated, you would be filled not only with pity for them, but with shame. Do you think, citizens, that young men who have taken this oath can be made soldiers? Are they to be trusted with arms when they leave this obscene sanctuary? Are they, defiled by their own and others' sins, to fight in defence of the honour of your wives and children? Every offence prompted by lust, deceit or violence which has been committed in these last years, originated in that shrine. The Evil grows every day. It affects the whole Commonwealth of Rome.'

The consul goes on to say that the will of the gods had been made a pretext for crime, and there is no question that he was right. The extensive prosecutions which followed show that the citizens made some differentiation between the orthodox worship of their deities and novel innovations too obviously made from purely human motives.

54

The *Bacchanalia* described above was a debased form of the Greek Dionysia. The Romans were more sophisticated than the Greeks, but it was this very sophistication that undid them. With the change of racial attitude, orgiastic behaviour became, not a purgative, but a habit-forming drug, and with the Roman attitude towards sexuality the nature of the god's influence on the proceeding, took on a new and sinister significance.

Whatever the cause, prosecutions undoubtedly followed involving about seven thousand persons. Many were executed, and still more attempted to flee from Rome in an attempt to avoid unwelcome publicity and criminal proceedings. Finally, when it was thought that the trouble had been satisfactorily eradicated, a senatorial decree was issued—186 B.C.—which has come down to us in the form of a bronze tablet, and which prohibits for ever the *Bacchanalia* throughout Rome and Italy. A few minor exceptions would be made, but the praetor was to be informed in advance.

The authorities did not intervene in the activities of the Bacchanalians from moral motives, but because they distrusted and refused to tolerate the existence of any rival organized body which might prove a potential menace to the power of the state.

The *Bacchanalia* started as a harmless vineyard cult, the sexual element was always present and inevitably, as can be seen in countless other instances, came to dominate the whole: a useful rationalization and mystification of purely human emotions, which placed on the shoulders of the deity the responsibility for the actions of the Bacchanalians which the lifting of their inhibitions, itself facilitated by the use of a deistic scapegoat, had released. The gods had become masters instead of friends.

Nowhere had the *Bacchanalia* caught on so rapidly, and perhaps from no other quarter had they so exerted their influence on the citizens of Rome, than Etruria. The Etruscans had long been known as a people easy-going in their morality and passionately addicted to luxury.

Athenaeus of Nauclia had commented on their society and on their banquets. Writing of the latter he remarks (*Deipnosophistae* IV 39) on their couches exquisitely embroidered with flowers and on their heavy silver drinking cups.

Later in the book (XIII 517) he gives further particulars:

'Among the Etruscans, who had become extravagantly luxurious, Timaeus records in his first book that the slave girls wait on the men naked. And Theopompus, in the forty-third book of his *Histories*, says that it is customary with the Etruscans to share their women in common; the women bestow great care on their bodies and often exercise even with the men, sometimes also with one another; for it is no disgrace for women to show themselves naked. Further, they dine, not with their own husbands, but with any men who happen to be present, and they pledge with wine any whom they wish. They are also terribly bibulous, and are very good-looking. The Etruscans rear all the babies that are born, not knowing who is the father in any single case. These in turn pursue the same mode of life as those who have given them nurture, having drinking parties often and consorting with all the women. It is no disgrace for the Etruscans to be seen doing anything in the open, or even having anything done to them; for this also is a custom of their country. And so far are they from regarding it as a disgrace that they actually say, when the master of the house is indulging in a love-affair, and someone inquires for him, that he is undergoing so and so, openly calling the act by its indecent name. When they get together for companionship or in family parties they do as follows: first of all, after they have stopped drinking and are ready to go to bed, the servants bring in to them, the lamps being still lighted, sometimes female prostitutes, sometimes very beautiful boys, sometimes also their wives; and when they have enjoyed these the servants then introduce lusty young men, who in their turn consort with them. They indulge in love-affairs and carry on these unions sometimes in full view of one another, but in most cases with screens set up around the beds; the screens are made of latticed wands over which cloths are thrown. Now they consort very eagerly, to be sure, with women; much more however, do they enjoy consorting with boys and striplings. For in their country these latter are very good-looking, because they live in luxury and keep their bodies smooth. In fact all the barbarians who live in the west remove the hair of their bodies by means of pitch plasters and by shaving with razors. Also, among the Etruscans at least, many shops are set up and artisans arise for this business, corresponding to barbers among us. When they enter these shops, they offer themselves unreservedly, having no modesty whatever before spectators or passers-by. This custom is also in use even among many of the Greeks who live in Italy; they learned it from the Samnites and the Messapians. In their luxury, the Etruscans, as Alcinous records, knead bread, practise boxing, and do their flogging to the accompaniment of the flute.'

That Bacchic dances were known in Etruria, apart from seeming in itself probable after reading the commentary above, is confirmed by one of the many wall-paintings left us at Tarquinia, Chiusi and other places. According to the author of *Etruria Past and Present*—M. A. Johnstone—in 'The Tomb of the Inscriptions' at Tarquinia there is a painting of 'some frenzied Bacchic dancing'. . . . 'The dancers are naked or nearly so, wear high long-toed boots always, and occasionally a loin-cloth, a jacket, a necklace or a wreath-decked hat, and carry a garland or two wherewith to enhance the rhythm of their gestures. Servants bearing the vessels of the wine-feast mix with the dancers and do a step or two themselves. Music is supplied from the double pipes, as it is also for the wrestling and boxing groups depicted in one corner of the room.'

Another tomb—'The Tomb of the Leopards'—'is named after the pair of hunting leopards which fill the pediment. Underneath them are the festive couches, which are here occupied in each case by a youth and a maiden, an arrangement which has aroused much controversy.'

The chief interest of this account lies in the fact that it shows the half-way house between Greek and Roman civilizations.

Allied to the *Bacchanalia*, but considerably more unsavoury, are the rites, plainly psycho-neurotic in origin, associated with the worship of *Cybele*.

Self-flagellation ostensibly for religious motives is a feature of more than one religious creed. In the worship of *Cybele*, the origin of this practice in the extreme form, is displayed. Behind this, although not behind all religious masochistic practice, lies the idea that morality is only compatible with a passive role in life and particularly in sexual life. That passive or female equals good and that aggressive or masculine equals bad, that masculinity must be sacrificed if oneself and others are to be saved, and sexuality even semi-consciously to remain acceptable. This idea is the stronger and more ineradicable for being linked to the sexual instinct and driven by its perpetual power. It was a neurosis that the priests of *Cybele* carried to its logical conclusion. It is possibly significant that the sudden rise of the cult occurred at the period towards the end of the Hannibalic war, when the nation was broken down by the long ardours of the campaign and the disasters which they wrought. The priests of *Cybele* were eunuchs. They followed the legend of Attis, who castrated himself in a frenzy for the sake of the young goddess whom he loved. The story can be read in Ovid.

> Attis, the lovely boy of the Phrygian forest,
> bewitched the goddess with the crown of towers.
> To keep him for herself, her temple-guardian,
> she said "Canst thou not always be a boy?"
> He gave his pledge, and said "If I am perjured,
> by an embrace, may it be my last love."
> But he was perjured, and gave up his boyhood
> in a nymph's arms. The goddess took revenge.
> She hacked the tree, and with it killed the Naiad,
> for with the tree the Naiad lived and died.

But Attis, mad, thinking the roof was falling,
rushed out, and ran to Dindyma's high peak,
crying "Ah the torches!" crying "Scourges!"
swearing the furies drove him to his death.
And now with a sharp stone he cut his body,
dragging his long hair in the filthy dust,
and crying "I deserve to bleed and suffer!
Perish the member that made me forsworn!
Away with it!" he cut away his manhood . . .
leaving no sign to show he once was male.
His madness still is copied, and his servants
cut their vile bodies while they toss their hair.

The worship of *Cybele*, besides involving self-castration in a state of frenzy, and dedication of the severed organs to the goddess, had also, as an important part of the ritual, a baptism by blood which came, appropriately enough, from a bull or ram. Banquets were given in honour of this goddess at private houses, but the actual consummation of her worship appears to have been performed by the priests alone. According to Apuleius, the priests of *Cybele* also indulged in homosexual practices with strong young peasants. Nevertheless and in spite of the opinions of Bloch, I cannot help believing that the chief significance of the cult lies along the lines I have indicated. The Greeks certainly practised flagellation in connexion with religious cults—but the idea of guilt was absent. (Note in the above 'I *deserve* to bleed and suffer.')

Isis was the female fertility goddess of crops and cultivation in Egypt. She was imported into Rome like many another deity, and like them transformed. Fertility, although obviously connected with sexuality, is opposed to, rather than connected with, prostitution. Yet temple prostitution played an important part in the worship of this goddess. I will not repeat a point I have already made too often.

The cult was received unfavourably by the authorities, being, possibly significantly, first recognized under Caligula.

Even Tiberius had an effigy of the goddess pulled from her shrine and pitched into the Tiber because the priests had used the ceremonies to dishonour a noble lady. The sexual element in this religion was indubitably flagrant. Ovid says: 'Do not ask what could happen in the temple of linen-clas Isis'; and elsewhere: 'Do not shun the temples of Isis, she makes many women become what she became for Jupiter.' Juvenal, always a straightforward and economic writer, calls the priestesses of *Isis* simply 'Bawds'. Kiefer, whilst admitting the probable truth of the accusations, says that 'of course, the priests and priestesses may very often have assisted in furthering such adventures (i.e. sexual ones) . . . as the priests of the Mighty Mother sometimes exhausted their passion in sexual frenzies, but all this has nothing to do with the cult, or with the real nature of the gods.' But unless we accept the existence of *Isis* herself as an absolute and literal fact, where are we to seek for the nature of the cult if not in the behaviour of its priests and priestesses? Kiefer's point seems to be so academic as to be incomprehensible. It is true that the worship of the goddess often required a period of sexual abstinence, which Kiefer quotes in support of his theory, but abstinence for what purpose if not for eventual release of accumulated desire?

Allied to the cult of *Isis* was that of the *Bona Dea*—the good goddess. She was, according to some, strictly a woman's goddess whose worship was conducted by women alone. At the celebration of her rites the master of the house would go out for the evening leaving the women alone. The lady of the house takes over the arrangements for the celebrations which involve 'gaiety and music'. So Plutarch. The picture painted by Juvenal is rather different. He has earlier bewailed the decay of Roman religions, blaming this on the drunken emancipation of the women.

'What decency does Venus observe when she is drunken? When she knows not one member from another, eats giant oysters at midnight, pours foaming unguents into her unmixed Falernian, and drinks out of perfumed bowls while the roof spins dizzily round, the table dances, and every light shows double!

Go to now, and wonder what means the sneer with which Tullia sniffs the air, or what Maura whispers to her ill-famed foster-sister, when she passes by the ancient altar of chastity. It is there that they set down their litter at night, and before the image of the goddess playing their filthy pranks for the morn to witness.'

Now he continues; describing the scenes that took place when the female worshippers of the *Bona Dea* had been left alone in the house.

'The rites of the Good Goddess! Shrieking flutes excite the women's loins, wine and the trumpet madden them, whirling and shrieking, rapt by Priapus. Then, then, their hearts are blazing with lust, their voices stammer with it, their wine gushes in torrents down their soaking thighs. . . . This is no mimicry, the thing is done in earnest: even Priam's aged loins and Nestor cold with age would burn to see it. Their itching cannot bear delay: this is sheer Woman, shrieking and crying everywhere in the hall, "It is time, let in the men!" The lover sleeps . . . then let him snatch a greatcoat, hurry here. No? Then they rush upon the slaves. Not even slaves? Then a scavenger comes off the streets.'

And if no man can be found; they content themselves with an ass, ends Juvenal. He often tends towards the most scurrilous interpretation of any set of circumstances, yet if the goddess were entirely the respectable figure painted by Bachofen, who would have thought of relating such tales? 'No smoke without fire' is an unsavoury slogan, but nevertheless it is frequently a reliable guide. Kiefer may indignantly deny the accusations against *Isis* and the *Bona Dea*. In comparison with *Cybele* and the *Bacchanalia* their worship was healthy, harmless and singularly free from multiple neurosis and perversion. But already all of them had become a game.

So far we have been examining national cults which resulted in, or were connected with, activities coming under the heading of orgies. In most people's minds a different picture is formed by the use of this word when applied to the Romans. A picture of the luxurious banquets of private individuals, in particular, imperial individuals, and the allegedly decadent effects and significance of these social activities. It is certain that the increase in luxury, or as some would have it, effeminacy, had a direct bearing on the cession of military activities. On the other hand, I think it would be misleading to ascribe the existence of this luxury to any more sinister or complicated cause than that the people were left with a lot of money and too little to do. Whether this was altogether a bad thing is to be doubted. There are many more objectionable pastimes than taking an elaborate concern in one's personal appearance, comfort and cleanliness, and amongst these I would certainly include military activity, particularly military activity of the kind practised by the Romans. What we have to decide is whether there was anything particularly corrupt, sinister and decadent about the Romans indulging themselves in this way or whether the Empire would have collapsed just as surely if the Romans had, for example, spent too much time playing golf.

At first sight I confess I see nothing but good. Nothing but an indulgence in harmless and simple pleasures, nothing sinister, no signs of the usual ubiquitous neurosis; unless the passion for baths can be taken as a symptom of a national guilt complex.

The newly acquired sophistication on the part of the Romans was due in large measure to Greek influence. The Coan garments mentioned in the chapter on the Greeks were imported into Rome in large quantities. They copied the Greek enthusiasm for nude statues. Their attitude towards nudity in the form of flesh or stone was cruder and less sensitive, in fact the total reverse of the Greek, as the Roman word for naked—*nudus*—shows. (The word has alternative meanings of: 'rough', 'uncouth', etc.) Since nudity and fashion are so closely related, the balance between what is revealed and what is concealed playing an important part in the arousal of sexual excitement, it is surprising that the Romans, like the Greeks, had no fashions as we understand the word. Apart from various innovations in colour in the Imperial period, the clothes remained static in design. There was, it must be added no orthodox style of draping the garments, and variations were thus possible within a limited frame.

Jewellery was luxurious and heavy. The consort of the Emperor Caligula possessed jewels worth, at a modern valuation, £1,200,000. The mistress of Trimalchio could be seen laden with jewellery weighing 6 lb. Jewels frequently bore the portrait of the current Emperor. Men who indulged in this piece of sycophancy had to have their wits about them, for a number of actions could be construed as treasonable. To pick up a chamber-pot with a hand bearing such a ring could be made a capital offence. Juvenal writes of *auratae papillae*, meaning gilded breasts, although it is not certain whether we should understand that women actually painted their breasts gilt, or that they wore a great number of gold ornaments on their breasts.

The hair was always elaborately arranged, and sometimes blonde hair from the heads of German girls was used to supplement or replace the black Mediterranean hair of the Romans. The Empress Messalina wore such a wig.

The elaborate and frequent bathing which was such a feature of Roman life was naturally accompanied by the construction of magnificently equipped baths. Martial speaks of such a bath. 'Oppianus, if you have not bathed in Etruscus' baths you die unbathed.' The walls of this palatial bath were inlaid with green marble mixed with a sort of alabaster; and besides the steamrooms there were basins into which water flowed from the Apennine mountains, brought in the channel constructed by Marcus Titus.

The baths in the city were a well-known rendezvous for clandestine lovers, and seem to have been generally associated, at any rate in the minds of the prudish, with licentiousness and immorality of every kind. There were also, according to

Martial, special baths for prostitutes, which were visited by no respectable woman, but which *were* visited by men. Mixed bathing was introduced at the time of the elder Pliny. The women alone wore bathing costumes, 'objectionable incidents naturally followed.'

Outside Rome, was Baiae, a famous watering place noted for its hot springs and its immorality. Seneca uttered a stern puritanical warning against the dangers of this place, speaking of 'drunk men wandering along the beach, banquets in boats, the lakes echoing with the voices of singers, and other acts of debauchery displayed as though the laws had ceased to bind them' and asking 'do you think Cato would ever have lived in one of these houses to count the adulterous women sailing past him, to hear the noise of singing every night.' In spite of his disapproving rhetoric Seneca only succeeds in producing a distinctly attractive picture of Baiae, a pleasant refuge from the noise, filth, and continual traffic of the great city, where the villas of the rich provided an agreeable retreat . . . for the rich.

Not all the pleasures of the city were provided by the gladiators and the other crudities of the arena. Theatrical performances and dancing were both popular, and a strong element of eroticism existed in both these forms of entertainment. They could be seen in private houses as well as in public places. Specially renowned for their skill in dancing of a lascivious nature were dancing girls from Cadiz, and at private banquets these girls often appeared to round off the evening's entertainment. Juvenal says of them:

> Perhaps you will expect the itching dances
> of Gades, while a band croons, and the girls
> sink to the ground and quiver to applause . . .
> a stimulus for languid lovers, nettles
> to whip rich men to life. . . .

and Martial:

> She trembles, quivers, sways her loins, and wriggles . . .
> She'd make Hippolytus forget himself.

64

Roman banquets were remarkable by any modern standards for the enormous quanties of food and drink consumed by the guests. The elegance of the Greek was totally lacking, and it was considered an accomplishment to be able to vomit at will in order that the process of eating might be started all over again. . . . *Vomunt ut edant, edunt ut vomant.* . . . Owing to the habit, prevalent at any rate among the faster set, of drinking wine neat instead of diluting it, intemperance was proportionately higher. The diner frequently became too drunk even to urinate successfully into a chamber-pot or wine vessel without the aid of the guiding hand of his slave. The debauches lacked nothing in splendour but everything in taste. The Romans either wilfully disregarded or failed to appreciate the need for the element of grace and dignity which most human beings find in one degree or another an indispensable part of their pleasures.

What is particularly disquieting in the Roman life of pleasure is not that it was confined to a minority of the rich, which has been and is the case in other societies, but that a basic part of the pleasure derived by the rich depended on this prerogative. The slave-based society is nowhere more clearly and repellingly revealed than at the dinners of the great, where a majority was bullied and humiliated, undergoing wretchedness for the sake of the pleasure of a few. If the aristocrats had derived any real pleasure from their excesses, our judgement on the Romans might be less harsh. They did not, and it is not. The Romans remain intriguing but completely hatable. Their pleasure was the antithesis of true Hedonism: based on the misery and defeat of Rome's own citizens and of those of the rest of Europe: as such it only could, and did in fact, fail.

As regards particular banquets and orgies, we naturally know more of those given by famous men than of those of nonentities. Obvious among the famous are the great Caesars. This method of examining the habits of the age is open to the objection that the Julian house was afflicted by a recurring streak of epilepsy, suffered from other, more severe abnormalities caused by too much intermarriage, and cannot be taken as representative of the period. To this I would reply that I do not think that one should expect to find in the pattern of orgies anything other than an isolated phenomenon, which cannot *necessarily* be linked to any other form of history. But that the insanity of the Julian house, if in the strictly medical sense it existed, was not so hereditary that it did not find an answering echo in the hearts of others, and this similarity cannot be attributed entirely to sycophancy. The neurosis of the Roman people, or at any rate of the ruling classes, was essentially connected, as in National Socialist Germany, with the identification of themselves with the state. The Emperor was the personification of the state, as not only others but also he himself would be aware. Is it then so irrelevant to examine the private or semi-private lives of these men?

Suetonius . . . 'that jackdaw of gossip' as Kiefer pettishly calls him, said that Julius Caesar was generally held to spend much energy and money on his lusts, and to have seduced many women of high rank. This is dismissed by Kiefer, who states (untruthfully) that these accusations were unsupported by more detailed evidence; as 'mere gossip'. Suetonius does, in fact, give a list of such women, and Kiefer's case is not made more impressive by the fact that having indignantly dismissed Suetonius' statements he goes on to add, 'besides, are we the better off for knowing that the great man gave his love to this or that woman outside the confines of marriage?' Most people would reply 'yes' if they answered this question sincerely, as obviously the private life of any public figure is just as much, if not rather more, a part of him than those aspects of his personality which he does choose to reveal. However, Kiefer must be granted that few details of Caesar's sexual life are available, and that he was probably much occupied by his military affairs. In Caesar the epilepsy of the Julian house first appeared in recurring attacks.

Augustus possessed the characteristic, unusual in his family, of being, so far as anybody could see, exclusively heterosexual in his sexual tastes. The originator of the marriage laws, he was himself no puritan. Roman Emperors did not expect to encounter difficulties where the satisfying of their particular lusts were concerned, and it is related of Augustus that he once called the wife of an ex-consul into a bedroom from her husband's dining-room, and brought her back with her ears still red and her hair ruffled. It is not an endearing story, but remembering that the Roman idea of marriage was very different from the Greek, and still more different, in spite of a superficial similarity, from any modern equivalent, one must temper one's judgement accordingly.

Augustus was also reputed to employ procureurs, who roamed the town 'stripping and inspecting women as if the whoremonger Toranius had been selling them.' He developed an obsessional predeliction for virgins (compare the eighteenth century in England) and even obtained the co-operation of his wife in procuring a steady and increasingly frequent supply. He seems to have satisfied his sexual voracity more or less in private, and there are no particular details of debauches given, or alleged to have been given by him, with the doubtful exception of 'The Dinner of the Twelve Gods' of which Suetonius says: 'At this the guests appeared in the guise of gods and goddesses, while he himself was made up to represent Apollo, as was charged not merely in the letters of Antony, who spitefully gives the names of all the guests, but also in these anonymous lines which everybody knows:

"As soon as that table of rascals had secured a Choragus, and Mallia saw six gods and six goddesses while Caesar impiously plays the false role of Apollo, and feasts amid novel debaucheries of the gods; then all the deities turned their faces from the earth and Jupiter himself fled from his golden throne." '

This banquet caused resentment as well as scandal, for there was at the time a serious famine, and the news of this piece of indulgence on the part of the Caesar was greeted by the cry that 'the gods had eaten all the grain!' and that Caesar was in fact Apollo, but Apollo the Tormentor, a surname under which the god was worshipped in one part of the city.

The nature or character of an individual long dead will always be a subject of dispute, and such a controversy exists around the person of Tiberius. On the one hand we have the picture of him, painted by Marañon, weak-willed and sexually timid, being divorced from his own, pregnant, wife, and marrying at the instance of Augustus the lecherous, enigmatic, half-crazed Julia, who had already, in spite of her enormous reputation for immorality, succeeded in attracting general attention by the vigour and enthusiasm with which she attempted to seduce him, Tiberius. How does this picture of Tiberius, still in love with Vispania, his first wife, and unmoved by the excitement of possessing the profligate princess which any other Roman would have felt, fit in with the account of the Emperor at the period of his residence at Capri, with his twelve palaces and his blue Grotto, indulging in the varied and uninhibited pleasures described by Suetonius. If Tiberius was as genuinely sensitive and retiring a man as some authors have attempted to make him out, what would be the effect on him of Julia's frantic preoccupation with copulation, of her endless affairs with men of every age, colour and class and of her eventual and literal prostitution? Was he a natural cynic or was he turned into one by his experiences? Or was he never sensitive or inhibited, never in love with Vispania, always a lecher, the change being from secret to open immorality?

Marañon thinks that he was not a chaste man by temperament but only by the necessity caused by his sexual timidity. He bases this belief partly on the long period (seven or eight years) during which Vispania failed to conceive, and the fact that after his breach with Julia, 'this man of thirty-two renounced all sexual activity.' How he deduces this renunciation apart from the absence of contemporary gossip, Marañon does not say. Yet when we *do* come to gossip relating to Tiberius' activities at Capri, these are dismissed as scurrilous nonsense. In further support of his hypothesis Marañon adduces the fact that Tiberius was tall and left-handed, both these physical characteristics being, according to him, well-known symptoms of sexual timidity and/or impotence. It is perfectly true that specific accusations were only made against him towards the end of his life. These accusers were the much-abused Suetonius and his fellow historian Dio(n) Cassius. Suetonius, who cannot be accepted simply in the light of a scandalmonger, says that 'Having gained the licence of privacy (i.e. at Capri) and being as it were out of sight of the citizens, he at last gave free rein at once to all the vices which he had for a long time ill-concealed.' This version is not so completely irreconcilable with Marañon's as Marañon would have us suppose. Many men and women who in public are sexually inhibited, behave quite differently when withdrawn from their usual surroundings and from the sight of their friends, their timidity being based only on a feeling that sexual activity is something which should be kept in a different compartment from the rest of their lives. Suetonius says that Tiberius was a great boozer, that he spent a night and two whole days feasting with two men, who were subsequently rewarded with the Governorship of Syria, and the Prefectship of the city. He was given a dinner by Cestius Gallius, 'a lustful and prodigal old man', and insisted that his host 'should change or omit none of his usual customs' and that nude girls should wait on them at dinner. He established a new office—'Master of the Imperial Pleasures'—and gave this to Titus Priscus, a Roman Knight.

At his retreat in Capri he devised an apartment with seats and couches in it, and 'adapted to the secret practice of abominable lewdness' where he entertained companies of girls and catamites whom he called 'Spintriae' and who defiled one another in his presence '*triplici serie conexi*' in order to arouse his flagging powers. He had bedchambers in many places decorated with pictures and sculptures. In these rooms were provided the books of Elephanti 'that none might want a pattern for any lewd project that was proscribed him.' In the woods were groves and recesses where 'young persons of both

69

sexes prostituted themselves in caves and hollow rocks dressed in the costumes of Sylvans and Nymphs.' In the Blue Grotto he swam like an old shark amongst a shoal of naked little boys, of an age when 'they were already fairly strong but had not yet been weaned.' 'These he called "his little fishes" and trained them to play between his thighs while he was bathing, to excite him little by little with their tongues and bites,' indulging, according to rumour, in other still less innocuous submarine activities.

What are we to make of these conflicting reports? Suetonius, whose reliability as an historian had better be examined here, was not, whatever his accusers may say, a scandalmonger or a pornographer. His prose style is flat and matter-of-fact; he sometimes, though not always, examines the rival claims of conflicting reports; his other works suggest that he was a serious scholar. His statements have in many cases been confirmed by other authorities. Bearing this in mind, is it likely that he would have invented a totally and, consequently, ludicrously improbable story about a man, not so long dead, who had been noted for his sexual timidity? Marañon suggests that this was a 'punitive legend' created by a society which hated him for other reasons. The legend of Capri is rejected by him 'on psychosexual grounds'. I am not convinced by either of these criticisms. If people wish to make an attack on a political enemy, they will either attack him on political grounds or they will choose a suitable alternative. They will not be so inept as to sacrifice totally plausibility to spectacularity.

After the contradictions and complexities of Tiberius, who was undoubtedly potentially, although just possibly not actually, sadistic and sexually depraved, it is a relief, if that is the right word, to turn to so obviously and undisputedly evil, tormented and psychopathic a figure as Caligula.

At an early age he committed incest, probably preceded by rape, with one of his sisters, Drusilla, to whom he remained devoted, after his fashion, for the remainder of her life. Whether this incest should be taken as a cause or as a result of his mental unbalance is problematic—there can be no doubt that he was, during the major portion of his reign, completely off his head.

When Drusilla died he issued a decree making it a capital offence during the period of mourning, for anyone to laugh, bathe, or eat a meal with parents, spouse, or children.

His other sisters he did not love, but prostituted to whom he chose. In his sexual, as in his public life, he displayed a strong sadistic trait. If he took a fancy to a woman, he removed her from her husband without the least hesitation; as in the case of the woman Paulina, whom, having obtained in this manner, he used for a short time and then dismissed, forbidding her upon pain of death, ever to have intercourse with anybody again. He displayed Caesonia, 'although she was neither beautiful nor young', naked to his friends, marrying her only when she was about to give birth to his child.

On criminals and the Roman population alike he inflicted the physical and mental cruelties dictated to him by his more than half-crazed brain. Convicted felons he fed alive to the lions, and no one, even among his immediate entourage, was immune from the constant danger of death by torture. Once, at a banquet, he suddenly burst into immoderate laughter, and when the consuls who were near him politely asked the reason, he replied, 'Because if I nodded once I could have all your throats cut.' He combined childishness with a devilish refinement in the tortures which he inflicted, particularly in the addition of mental to physical pain. He insisted that examinations by torture be conducted in his presence whilst he was banqueting, and when once at a dinner a slave was caught stealing a strip of silver, Caligula gave orders that his hands should be cut off and hung about his neck, together with a placard giving the reason for his punishment, and that he should then be led about the room. At banquets, he would invite women in whom he was interested, taking care always to invite their husbands as well, and then, as they passed by the foot of his couch, 'he would inspect them critically and deliberately as though buying slaves, even putting out his hand and lifting up the face of anyone who looked down in modesty: then, as often as the fancy took him, he would leave the room, sending for the one who pleased him best, and returning soon afterwards with evident signs of what had occurred, he would openly commend or criticize his partner, recounting her charms or defects, and commenting on her conduct. To some he sent a bill of divorce in the name of their absent husbands and had it entered in the public records . . . there was scarcely any woman of rank he did not approach.'

'Many men of honourable rank were first disfigured with the marks of branding-irons and then condemned to the mines, to work at building roads or to be thrown to the wild beasts; or else he shut them up in cages on all fours like animals, or had them sawn asunder. Not all these punishments were for serious offences, but merely for criticizing one of his shows, or for never having sworn by his Genius. He forced parents to attend the executions of their sons, sending a litter for one man who pleaded ill-health, and inviting another to dinner immediately after witnessing the death, and trying to rouse him to gaiety and jesting by a great show of affability.'

'In reckless extravagance he outdid the prodigals of all times in ingenuity, inventing a new sort of baths and most unnatural varieties of food and feasts, for he would bathe in hot or cold perfumed oils, drink pearls of great price dissolved in vinegar, and set before his guests loaves and meats of gold.'

'He built Liburnian galleys with ten banks of oars, with sterns set with gems, particoloured sails, huge spacious baths, colonnades and banqueting halls, and even a great variety of vines and fruit trees; that on board of them he might recline at table from an early hour and coast along the shores of Campaian amidst songs and choruses.'

He constructed innumerable houses and villas regardless of expense, and with a marked predilection for building sites in inaccessible and ludicrous positions. Artificial mountains were built on plains. The tops of existing mountains were sliced off. Rocks were constructed in the sea where none had been before, all these operations being conducted at lightning speed to satisfy the passing whim of the Emperor.

He raised the money necessary for these operations by conducting auction sales at which those present were compelled to buy, at fantastic expense, objects for which they had not the smallest desire.

He invented grotesque and novel taxes, on food, on lawsuits and even on prostitutes, 'providing that those who had ever been prostitutes should be liable to this public tax, and that even matrimony should not be exempt.'

'To leave no kind of plunder untried, he opened a brothel in his palace, setting apart a number of rooms and furnishing them to suit the grandeur of the place, where matrons and freeborn youths should stand exposed.' He then sent touts about the city, and to those who came, lent money at an extortionate rate of interest.

Caligula's chief obsession was with cruelty, and that of a kind so remotely connected with sexuality that we can only tentatively include it in our list. He was well aware of his own insanity, and in spite of his aggressiveness and childish conceit, or possibly as a cause of it, he was not insensitive to personal criticism. Tall, pale, with a balding head and an excessively hirsute body, he refused to allow anybody to look down on him from above or to use the word 'goat', and to do so was treated as a capital offence. He was tormented by insomnia and by hallucinations and was observed to dread the coming of darkness. His life was miserable, and by any standards odious, his abnormality is sufficiently great for us to leave him here.

Claudius, his successor, although undisputedly extremely fond of women, wine and food, does not seem to have combined his erotic and gastronomic pleasures. He was a strange, enigmatic figure, timid and studious in youth and with a constant and obsessional fear of deposition or assassination when he became Emperor. He is claimed to have shared Caligula's taste for having examinations by torture conducted

73

in his presence. His attitude towards the common people seems to have alternated between a show of force and spectacular gestures designed to gain him an easy popularity. He gave many large banquets, and at one such entertainment given on the banks of the canal to celebrate the draining of the Fucine lake he was very nearly drowned in company with his six hundred guests. He toyed at one time with the idea of issuing a special edict permitting farting and belching in his presence, having been told, and apparently believed, that one of his guests had nearly died through restraining himself from these actions. At his banquets, he frequently drank enormous quantities of undiluted wine until he passed out, flat on his back, snoring loudly. A feather would then be thrust down his throat 'in order to make him throw up the contents of his stomach'. He seems to have been regarded by his subjects as a rather ludicrous figure. He gave a great many public spectacles and died, it is said, of poison administered in a dish of mushrooms, to which he was inordinately addicted. At one time he was married to the fantastic Messalina, whose nymphomania must be regarded almost as psychopathic. She pursued with mechanical eagerness every man within sight, on those who failed to succumb she poured all the venomous ingenuity and spite that she could muster. She finally, after verbally applauding the notion of polygamy for women, married another man, Silius, whilst she was still married to Claudius, and collected round her a sort of fast set.

'In the meantime, Messalina, being intoxicated by her wild and disorderly pleasures, was in the house of Silius her new husband . . . she had assembled a troop of favourites and women as debauched as herself at a masquerade. They celebrated the feast of Bacchus with all the impure ceremonies and infamous gestures which were practised at the Bacchanalia.' This party went on for several days on end, and finally Claudius got wind of it, and came from Ostia to break it up.

Nero has been regarded by some as the archetype of

74

wickedness and as representative of all the evils which allegedly caused the collapse of the Roman Empire. Certainly he displayed a wide variety of undesirable characteristics, yet I think it would be wrong to regard him as essentially insane as Caligula, or as purely odious. He had the misfortune, which his subjects were compelled to share, to have been brought up in circumstances, and to have a heredity, which could not have failed to damage the life and happiness of anybody. Unfortunately for him, and for Rome, he was placed in a position where he could gratify any desire, however fantastic, and, being completely unable to recognize that not all the impulses which we experience are conducive to self-preservation, he plunged unheedingly towards disaster.

His ancestors on both sides were all tarred with the brush of sadism, but although this may be relevant in view of the streak of this perversion which Nero subsequently developed, the blame must rest chiefly on the dominating and obnoxious figure of his mother, under whose influence he was placed from the age of three to eleven. Nothing more was needed to complete the damage except the two things which were immediately supplied: the placing of Nero under the tutelage of the austere figure of Seneca, a man of feeble will and strong homosexual inclinations, who tutored him from the age of puberty to adolescence, when he was married to a girl chosen by his mother as being unlikely to inspire him with any enthusiasm, erotic or otherwise, which might prejudice her own influence over him.

No matter who, if anyone, can be held to blame, Nero was undoubtedly from an early age bi-sexual, and in this connexion it is relevant to quote a remark of Suetonius: 'I have heard from several sources that Nero was convinced that no one was chaste in any part of his or her body, and that most merely dissimulated their vice under a clever pretence.'

Early in his reign Nero, according to Tacitus, began to spend his nights in the most extraordinary pastimes. Dressed as a slave, he would sally forth into the more squalid quarters of the town, where ranging the streets, the brothels and the wine-shops, he would commit all sorts of assaults and thefts. At first he received a good deal of verbal and physical abuse as the result of this conduct, but finally it got about that the prankster was in fact the Caesar, and encouraged by this immunity he increased and extended his depredations into wider and bolder fields, committing sexual assault on both men and women. Needless to say, there was no shortage of opportunists who, realizing the possibilities of this unique situation, organized bogus gangs, and scavenged the streets, enjoying the immunity which the fear of the citizens afforded them. None dared to resist, for if they did so the penalty was death, or at best compulsory suicide, and few were ready to take the gamble by offering resistance to a suspected fraud.

Nero's homosexual tendencies were unmistakable and firmly rooted at an early age, but he was none the less a victim of his lust for women. In fact, according to Tacitus, the deterioration in Nero's character dates from the time when he was seized with a desire to possess the fashionable and infamous Sabina Poppaea. This beautiful, calculating and basically unpleasant woman he removed from her husband, the man who was later to become the Emperor Otho, and who had been carried away to sufficient heights of suicidal idiocy to praise his wife and her charms in the presence of the egocentric and all-powerful Emperor. Poppaea herself, the mistress of her emotions and knowing exactly what she wanted, would give in on one condition only: that she should be Empress of Rome. A struggle of incredible bitterness then ensued between those two harridans, Agrippina and Poppaea. The resemblance between the two was hardly coincidental, and when Suetonius remarked that Nero had chosen a prostitute to be his wife because she resembled his mother, there can be little doubt that he was on the right track. Poppaea came off victorious in the teeth of opposition, not only from Agrippina, but also from the people, who resented the overthrow of Octavia. She did not enjoy her victory for long. Three years later she died; Nero, or so it was said, having kicked her in a fit of childish rage whilst she was pregnant.

That Nero had powerful aesthetic leanings should not be doubted or ridiculed. It is the one pathetic feature of his life, and as his impulses remained incapable of sublimation, in spite of his frequent and ludicrous attempts at acting, dancing, singing, and playing on musical instruments, he was compelled to transform them into more attainable, if less satisfactory and artistically valuable forms.

The spectacles he gave in the arena were imaginative and extraordinary. He ceased to pursue his curious fantasies stealthily and by night, and took to banqueting in public in the arena of the Circus Maximum, waited on by all the whores of the town. He prolonged his revels from midday to midnight, refreshing himself in the intervals with hot baths in winter, or in the summer, baths chilled with snow. Whenever he sailed down the Tiber to Ostia, or coasted through the Gulf of Baiae, booths fitted out for debauchery were set out at intervals along the shore, at the doors of which stood matrons who, like bawds and hostesses, implored him to land. He would invite himself to dinner with his friends. At one such, four million sesterces were spent on roses alone. He raped a Vestal Virgin and castrated a male favourite, Sporus, 'even endeavouring to transform him into a woman.' With this gelded creature he went through a form of marriage, afterwards 'having him conducted like a bride to his own house and treating him as his wife.' . . . 'This Sporus he carried about with him in a litter round the solemn assemblies and fairs of Greece and afterwards in Rome through the Sigillaria, dressed in the rich attire of an Empress, kissing him from time to time as they rode together.'

'That he had an incestuous passion for his mother was accepted by all, and it was said that whenever he travelled with her in a litter he abandoned himself to this pleasure, as the stains on his clothing proclaimed.' The existence of such a relationship is supported by the stories of Tacitus and

77

Claudius Rufus (whose work, quoted by Tacitus, is now lost). He became, if Suetonius can be believed, more and more fanciful in the pursuit of his pleasures.

'He so prostituted his own chastity, that after defiling almost every part of his body, he at last devised a kind of game in which, covered with the skin of some wild animal, he was let loose from a cage and attacked the private parts of men and women, who were bound to stakes, and when he had sated his mad lust, was "dispatched" by his freedman Doryphorus; for he was even married to this man in the same way that he himself had married Sporus, going so far as to imitate the cries and lamentations of a maiden being deflowered.'

No one example of the sexual behaviour of the Romans is so significant and interesting as this. I would point out that here is substantiation of the suggestion that the sadism of the Romans had incorporated in it a masochistic and self-destructive element.

Men had travelled a long way from the days of Homeric Greece.

This aspect of his character appears also in another form, his frenzied and successful efforts to get rid of money as soon as he had it. He praised Caius, his uncle, for the speed with which he had succeeded in disposing of the fortune left to him, Caius, by Tiberius. His own expenses were almost unbelievable. In strange contrast, or perhaps balance to his sadistic impulses, he distributed money by lottery; throwing small metal balls to the crowd, which bore numbers entitling those who picked them up to money, slaves, animals, boats, houses and estates. He bestowed enormous monetary gifts on anybody who contrived to earn his capricious and whimsical approval. Shortly subsequent to a fire in Rome, which there is no evidence that Nero either engineered or applauded, he built his fantastic Golden House, chiefly, though not exclusively, remarkable for its enormous dimensions in every direction. A lake like the sea; gardens containing wild and tame animals; a statue of himself 120 feet high; dining-rooms 'with fretted ceilings of ivory, whose panels could turn and shower down flowers and were fitted with pipes for sprinkling the guests with perfumes. The main banquet-hall was circular and constantly revolved night and day like the heavens. . . . In the rest of the house all parts were overlaid with gold and adorned with gems and mother-of-pearl.' The vestibule containing the statue of the Emperor was so immense that 'it had a triple colonnade a mile long.'

Violence and megalomania played an increasingly more important part in his life, until at the age of thirty-one he was compelled to commit suicide, which after much procrastination he at length accomplished with the help of his secretary, in order to avoid being flogged to death, the penalty which the senate had decreed for him.

The organizer of Nero's pleasures is thought to have been Petronius, the author of the Satyricon, and who was described by Tacitus as: 'A man who passed his days in sleep and his nights in the ordinary duties and recreations of life. Unlike most who walk the road to ruin he was never regarded as either debauchee or wastrel, but rather as the finished artist in extravagance.'

If this was the case, as the nature of the Satyricon tends to confirm, it is surprising that Nero's pleasures were not of a more subtle, sophisticated nature. Petronius had no very good opinion of Nero: he aroused the jealousy of Tigellinus, than whom he had proved a better professor of debauchery, and was compelled to commit suicide. In his will he described the Emperor's enormities, added a list of his catamites, his women and his innovations in lasciviousness; then sealed the document, sent it to Nero, and broke his signet ring to prevent it from being used to endanger others.

Vitellius, a man much addicted to eating and drinking, and who had acquired the knack of vomiting at will in order to facilitate his indulgences, possessed that fondness for cruelty, for the horrors of the arena, for the witnessing of examinations by torture, which we are no longer surprised to encounter after even a short acquaintance with the Romans. He had spent his boyhood and early youth with Tiberius at Capri, 'being branded for all time with the nickname Spintria.'

A great gastronome, he invented a dish called 'The Shield of Minerva'. This dish consisted of a mixture of the livers of parrot-fish, the brains of pheasants and peacocks, the tongues of flamingoes and the entrails of lampreys. Of his sexual habits we know little. He was killed in circumstances of the utmost cruelty.

Domitian is a more interesting if depressingly morbid figure. Suetonius says that at first he had a horror of shedding blood, although in the early part of his reign he used to seclude himself for an hour daily; which time he passed in catching flies and stabbing them with a sharp pin. A man so obviously morbid could not be expected long to confine himself to flies, and Domitian's cruelties were both subtle and excessive. He organized many public spectacles, particularly in the form of naval battles, and was a hard-working administrator of the law. He prohibited prostitutes from making use of litters, and punished the sexual immorality of the Vestal Virgins with death. In his private life he was quite inordinately over-sexed, being accustomed to refer, with revolting archness, to copulation as 'bed-wrestling'. He also, or so they said, was fond of depilating his concubines with his own hand, and would spend the long hours of the hot Italian afternoon lying on a bed indulging in this occupation. (It was the almost universal habit for women to remove their pubic hair by singeing or plucking.) He also used to swim with 'the very lowest prostitutes of the town' and was indirectly responsible for the death of his niece, whose pregnancy, caused by him, he had insisted that she attempt to terminate.

One interesting story concerning this Emperor, which appears nowhere else, but which is certainly well worth repeating, is told by Cassius Dio:

'Domitian had a room hung entirely with black—ceiling, walls and floor—and furnished with black benches without cushions. His guests were shown into this room at night, with no attendants. There was a slab of stone beside each of them, like a tombstone, bearing that guest's name; and the slabs were lit by the little lamps which are hung on tombs. Then there appeared beautiful boys, naked and painted black like spectres: they moved round the guests in an uncanny dance, and then stood one at the feet of each of the guests. Now food and drink were brought in, as for the banquet of the dead— all black and in black dishes. The guests shook with terror; they expected the death-blow to fall at any moment; the room was as silent as the grave; only Domitian spoke, and he talked only of murder and sudden death. At last he dismissed them. But before he did so, he sent away his servants who had been waiting in the courtyard so that the guests were carried or driven home by total strangers—which increased their terror. Finally, when they had all reached home and partially recovered, a messenger from the Emperor was announced. Every guest thought his last hour had struck. But instead, each of the guests received his gravestone (which was of silver) and then other gifts, including the valuable dishes of costly workmanship which had been set before him at the banquet and, finally, even the boy who played his wraith, now washed clean and beautifully dressed. These were their compensations for the death-agony they had suffered all the preceding night. Such were the feasts Domitian gave to celebrate his victories (as he said)—or rather (as the people said) in honour of those who lost their lives, both in Dacia and in Rome.'

Finally, to round off the list of Emperors, we will choose Heliogabalus, in whose extraordinary personality the erotic element in religion reaches its most exaggerated state.

This fourteen-year-old boy was, and remained, the priest of a cult which 'combined obscenity and mysticism without reconciling them.' When, as the result of the energy and unscrupulousness of his grandmother, he arrived at Rome, he attempted to introduce his own Syrian cult to the exclusion of all others. His deity is generally believed to have been Baal, the Syrian sun-god, whose strongly phallic element was exhibited in a statue at Emesa, which consisted of a large, black, phallo-conical stone. If any further evidence was required, there was the deity's temple at Rome, which was flanked by two colossal phalli.

Heliogabalus was said by Herodian, though the statement is certainly not borne out by coin portraits, to have been a remarkably beautiful youth. 'When he did sacrifice, and danced in the foreign way around the altar to the sound of flutes and pipes and other instruments, he took the eyes of all the men . . . especially of the soldiers, who knew that he was of royal birth.'

He wore costly and feminine clothes when celebrating the rites of his deity, which he did in the presence of the entire assembled Senate and all the knights of Rome. At these ceremonies he slaughtered an enormous number of animals, drenched their carcasses in scent, and to the noise of various musical instruments capered round the altar encircled by a troupe of Syrian girls. Human beings were also sacrificed on occasion, and the severed genitals of pubescent boys thrown into the sacrificial fire.

He conceived the ludicrous idea of marrying his deity to a goddess consort. Juno was favoured in this way and Heliogabalus himself celebrated the rites with suitable pomp.

In the summer, the deity changed his residence from one temple to another. This move took place on a jewelled chariot which he, the deity, drove himself. Heliogabalus ran backwards in front of the chariot the entire way, holding the horses' bits, and was himself supported by two soldiers.

He became more and more openly enamoured of his god, and it can be observed that the priests of a masculine cult often see themselves as feminine, as Heliogabalus certainly did. He married a Vestal Virgin, saying, 'it is the appropriate act of religion for a priest to wed a priestess', but he soon got rid of her, for his sexual tastes, as will have been guessed, lay elsewhere. He toyed with the idea of castrating himself, but finally settled for circumcision. At night he would go to a brothel, drive out the prostitutes, and wearing a wig stand in the door himself, soliciting trade. He later set aside a room in the palace in which he indulged in similar fantasies.

He tried to induce the physicians to make him into a woman, promising them large sums should they succeed. That there was a masochistic element in his character need not surprise us. According to Dio Cassius he liked to fantasize himself as a particularly lewd woman, taking pains to be caught *in flagrante delicto* by his 'husband' so that he should be severely beaten.

All this behaviour he doubtless regarded idealistically as a form of worship of his phallic god, which in a sense it was. All the same, his belief in his deity was on a different level to the Greek belief in Dionysos. He used it more consciously than any Greek as a means of expressing his sexual desires—and above all there is the element of masochism—i.e. the choice of the feminine role through feelings of *guilt* connected with the masculine.

His behaviour finally aroused the anger as well as the contempt of the army and the populace. He was murdered with his whole household and his body pitched into the Tiber.

The Romans, although the most spectacular, must also be considered the most contemptible people who have ever attempted the orgy-experiment. The reason for making this judgement I have outlined. With the exception of a few true Hedonists, such as Petronius, they had none of them any true understanding of the nature of pleasure. Lacking grace and elegance, contemptuously disposed towards the actions which they pretended to admire, it cannot be wondered if their behaviour has about it a suspicious odour of the death-wish. Present or no, this wish was presently consummated with the arrival of the Christian era. . . .

THREE

THE MIDDLE AGES AND THE RENAISSANCE

THE Romans, although their behaviour indicated a certain degree of guilt concerning the sadistic element in their culture, expended comparatively little on purely sexual misdemeanours. However, their sadism was bound up with sexual guilt, and in their culture we can see the first glimmerings of a new concept— the concept of sin.

Amid the ruins of the collapsing Empire there had started to expand a body of men with a new outlook on life, the continuation of those first few wisps of guilt, and these men and their successors proceeded to impose on the easy-going, semi-primitive people of Europe their own, highly restrictive code of behaviour, with results which nobody could call desirable. The European in the early part of the period enjoyed an extraordinary measure of sexual freedom, and the operation was a titanic failure.

At first society, not excluding the priests themselves, merely ignored the prohibitions, which were in fact, not strict. Then, as the Church stepped up its activity and as the patristic guilt-culture which it was trying to impose on a tolerant and matristic society began to take a hold, the sexual energy of the people was transformed into every kind of undesirable form of psychoneurotic behaviour—hysterical attacks, erotic illusions, incubi and succubi, witch-hunts and witchcraft (in that sequence), flagellomania, psychic impotence, etc. etc. etc. There continued to be, of course, those who ignored the prohibitions, but apart from the danger of legislative punitive action, such men probably tended to overreact against the Church and to be led into forms of behaviour in which they would otherwise not have engaged.

At the beginning of the period, as has been said, more or

less frank sexuality prevailed. The court records are full of convictions for sexual offences: fornication, adultery, incest and homosexuality. In the eighth century Boniface complained that: 'the English utterly despise matrimony, utterly refuse to have legitimate wives, and continue to live in lechery and adultery after the manner of neighing horses and braying asses.' Certainly there was a tendency to treat marriage in a light-hearted spirit—the married state being regarded as essentially temporary, and a husband or wife taken in the spirit of one ordering goods on approval. Virginity was regarded as of no great value, and bastardy by no means a disgrace, but rather as an honour, the implication being that some especially valiant knight had slept with one's mother. Aphrodisiacs were always in demand, even if belief in the efficacy of these was based, as in the case of the root of the orchis, which roughly resembled in shape the testicles, on the principle of sympathetic magic. Dress reflected the moral outlook, being quite fantastically indecent. Men wore a short coat which did not cover either the buttocks or the private parts—the latter being encased in a tight bag known as a braguette which served to accentuate rather than to conceal their shape. Women wore dresses very tight over the hips, and laced their breasts so high that 'a candle could be stood upon them'. Modesty in the usual sense of the word was unknown. In 610 the Queen of Ulster and the ladies of her court came to meet Cuchulainn naked above the waist, and raised their skirts 'so as to expose their private parts', thus indicating how deeply they honoured him. The teaching of the Church on sexual matters was not accepted by the medical profession who held that continence was unwise and unhealthy, and prescribed more frequent sexual intercourse to their patients. The Church in the early period was still taking a tolerant view of prostitution and appreciated its value—Aquinas said that prostitution was a necessary adjunct of morality—'a cesspool is necessary to a palace if the whole palace is not to smell.' Certainly the number of prostitutes was very large and more than one Church dignitary followed the example of the Bishop of Winchester and, treating prostitution as a sound financial investment, disregarded the moral side of the question; hence the euphemism 'Winchester Geese' for prostitutes.

The idea of the medieval knight as chivalrous, chaste, the respecter and helper of damsels in distress and in every way a perfect gentleman was one created by Christian and Victorian re-writers of history. Traill and Mann say: 'to judge from contemporary poems and romances, the first thought of every knight on finding a lady unprotected, was to do her violence'; and Gawain, the alleged paragon of knightly chivalry, raped Gran de Lis, despite her screams and struggles, when she refused an invitation to sleep with him. Celtic society remained, in spite of the prohibitions of the Church, essentially tolerant in its moral outlook and general character, and, as during the pre-Christian period, much of the running was made by women. Amazingly few of the clergy seemed able or willing to swallow their own medicine, and, like the sheep they sought to lead, they remained unpricked by guilt.

Archembald, Bishop of Sens in the tenth century, 'taking a fancy to the Abbey of St. Peter, drove out the monks and established a harem of concubines in the refectory and installed his hounds and hawks in the cloister.'

An unending stream of complaint met the attempts of the Church to enforce celibacy in its ministers. The parishioners of a priest would usually support him in his demands for a wife as otherwise, as they knew perfectly well, he would seek relief among their own wives. Henry III, Bishop of Liege, was known to have sixty-five illegitimate children, and in Germany '*pfaffenkind*' became a well-recognized word meaning 'bastard'. The *jus primae noctis* (which did undoubtedly exist in spite of allegations to the contrary, as Ducange has proved) was enforced by the monks of St. Thiodard over the inhabitants of St. Auriol. The pressure of the Church was applied without effect, and sexual energy continued to be disposed of steadily and successfully, and, moreover, at a somewhat startling rate.

But times were changing. The Hildebrandine reforms included ministers as well as monks in their demands for celibacy, and about this period a change for the worse occurs in the sexual health of the people. Abstinence from sexual activity leads to an almost total mental preoccupation with the subject, and psychoneurotic symptoms and sexual hallucinations were developed on a really astounding scale. A terrific outburst of incubi and succubi swept the bedrooms of Europe. These were nocturnal visitors, connected, in the minds of the Christians, with witchcraft and devilry, who indulged in liberties with the afflicted person, always of a sexual nature. They were particularly common in nunneries, and seemed also to be highly infectious.

Some idea of the true nature of these visitors may be obtained from the following story:

Goerres, a priest, was sent to exorcise a girl of twenty who had been pursued by an incubus. He reports:

'She told me, frankly, everything which the evil spirit had done to her. I thought, after hearing what she had to say, that in spite of her denials she had been giving the demon a sort of indirect consent. In fact she was always warned of its approaches by a violent excitement of the sexual organs; and then, instead of having recourse to prayer, she ran to her room and lay down on the bed. I tried to awaken in her a feeling of confidence in God, but with no success, and she seemed rather to be afraid of being delivered.' It is obvious that Goerres was no kind of fool; even by some contemporary physicians the origin of these phenomena was recognized or at least suspected, and Chaucer drily points out that since the appearance of the wandering friars (who had a reputation for promiscuous sexual behaviour with the wives of absent husbands) these visitors have become less common. But the general view of them was as diabolic phenomena. The existence of witches appeared as a natural supposition, and as a result the witch-hunting rage inevitably followed. The visitations of incubi were occasionally followed by phantom pregnancies.

For the stronger personalities among the supposedly celibate, there were numerous means of obtaining sexual gratification. The most common complaint against the priests in this connexion being that they sometimes used their power of withholding absolution to induce women to sleep with them. Another abuse to which a priest might put his profession was to compel a fornicator to name his partner, so that he might know where best to apply his own efforts. In their immorality the clergy always had the pattern set them right up the hierarchical scale, the Vicar of God himself seeming especially susceptible in this respect, for the list of Popes contains extensive examples. John XII turned St. John Latheran into a brothel. At his trial the charges included sacrilege, simony, perjury, murder, adultery and incest. Benedict IX, who was elevated at the age of ten, 'grew up in unrestrained licence, and shocked even the dull sensibilities of a gross and barbarous age by the scandals of his daily life.' Balthasar Cossa, later John XXIII, was tried and deposed confessing to 'notorious incest, adultery, defilement, homicide and atheism.' 'When, as Chamberlain to Boniface IX he had scandalized Rome by openly keeping his brother's wife as a concubine, the remedy adopted for the disorder was to create him Cardinal and send him as legate to Bologna where two hundred maids, matrons and widows, including a few nuns, fell victims to his brutal lust.' But we are advancing too fast.

Petrarch attacked Papal Avignon monotonously and at length. It was 'filled with every kind of confusion, the horror of darkness overspreading it, and it contained everything fearful which had ever existed, or been imagined by a disordered mind.' It out-Babyloned Babylon and 'men and places have the same appearance, obscene, ugly, horrible.'

To return to the period when the Church first began to succeed in implanting guilt in the minds of its flock. One of the results of this was an enormous outburst of Thanatic excess, disguised sexuality, turned inwards, and appearing in the form of orgies of self-flagellation, an unending attempt to out-balance guilt. These, by their number and obvious fascination for the participants, began to alarm the Church itself, which even through its own neurosis sensed something of the motives which lay behind this behaviour. Beginning with such mild enjoyments as hair-shirts, some devotees proceeded to the extreme of Christine of St. Troud who 'fastened herself upon a wheel, had herself racked, and hung on a gallows beside a corpse. Not content with this she even had herself partly buried in a grave.' There is scarcely an end to the nauseating manifestations of suppressed and transformed sexuality produced in the second half of the medieval period, and these are all directly attributable to the sexual 'morality' of the Church. Its objection to erotic pleasure lay simply in the fact that it was pleasurable, as is shown by the edicts of the Church concerning coital positions. (*Coitus a posteriori* was prohibited—not, as has been stated because it recalled the behaviour of animals, but because it causes too much satisfaction.) From the same attitude there arose the chemise cagoule—a kind of heavy nightshirt with a single, suitably placed hole through which, when it was necessary for the husband to impregnate his wife, copulation could be effected with the minimum possible contact and pleasure.

The flagellomaniac cult was exceedingly widespread, and is of sufficiently well-recognized a sexual origin to be classed unreservedly as orgiastic: 'The contagion spread very rapidly, extending as far as the Rhine provinces, and across Germany into Bohemia. Day and night a long procession of all classes and ages headed by priests carrying crosses and banners perambulated the streets in double file reciting prayers and drawing the blood from their bodies with leathern thongs. The magistrates in some Italian towns expelled the flagellants with threats and for a time the sect disappeared.'

Calamities such as earthquakes and the Black Death soon provided a further pretext for self-mortification and the flagellants reppeared. In 1349 Clement VI issued a Bull against the 'heresy' involved in self-flagellation but without noticeable success. Later a flagellant leader in Italy was burned at the stake.

The psychotic capers induced in the populace were performed mostly by the members of society with the weakest personalities. The stronger kept up a steady standard of rebellion, which finally prevailed, as we shall see. First I want to say something about these continuous, minority group, anarchic bodies and to describe their determined and stormy passage through the medieval gloom to the renaissance.

There were the heretics, whose persecution, although they were not strictly speaking moral rebels, can only be explained, considering the triviality of the points on which they differed from the orthodox, by the mother-fixated nature of their behaviour (particularly in the case of the troubadors), which one would naturally expect to prove repugnant to an authoritarian and patristic Church. (*See* G. Rattray Taylor, *Sex in History*, Thames and Hudson, 1953.) The resulting creed did not involve orgies, although the troubadors' idea of non-sexual devotion to one woman did not necessarily exclude sexual activity with others.

The Christian Church, it is very interesting to observe, retained as two of its principal festivals, two ex-pagan festivals—Christmas and Easter—both of which were originally connected with fertility. Thus it provided, part consciously, part unconsciously, a sort of safety-valve. The May Games and the Feast of Fools, although regarded with disfavour by the Church, were not suppressed by it, because it simply could not enforce its will concerning them.

These two ceremonies, although they certainly had their origin in pagan religion and embodied many features of their progenitors, the slinging of excrement, the transvestism, the general sexual licence, cannot be called religious in the true sense but should be regarded rather as an exaggerated kind of holiday, cathartic and orgiastic in character, but not taken too seriously by the participants.

More serious forms of phallus and fertility worship did

continue stealthily in spite of all efforts to stop them, and probably do still continue in the rural and primitive districts of Europe, although in the modern world fertility worship has been replaced by the cult of 'vitamin' and 'potency' pills, and other squalid and ineffectual idiocies of the Charing Cross Road.

The May Games, although probably taking place at this period, had not yet come into the open and will be dealt with later. The Feast of Fools was celebrated on the occasion of the Feast of the Circumcision, which corresponds to the Feast of Janus, but in no other way did it coincide with the activities of the Christian Church.

It was chiefly the affair of the minor clergy, true, but everything which they did in the way of celebration consisted of mockery and parody of the religion of which they were supposed to be priests.

The festival was centred in France, but even within the borders of this country a considerable variation was to be found in the ceremony.

At Beauvais, a donkey was introduced into the church, and the celebrant of the mass, instead of saying '*Ite missa est*' brayed three times. At St. Omer, a 'bishop' and a 'dean' of fools took part in the services. The latter was censed in a burlesque fashion, and the whole office was recited at the pitch of the voice and even with howls.

Naturally the superior clergy viewed the exotic horseplay of their subordinates with dislike and alarm. The protests, at first local, soon became national. In 1398 the Dean of Auxerre was complaining about the grants of wine made by the Chapter to the thirsty revellers, and two years later an order was passed to check various unseemly manifestations, including the beating of men and women through the streets.

In the same year Jean-Charlier de Gerson denounced the Feast of Fools, saying that 'the indecence of the Feast would shame a kitchen or a tavern.'

In 1445 the Faculty of Theology in the University of Paris

addressed a strong indictment of the Feast to the bishops, complaining that it clearly had its origins in paganism. They say:

'Priests and clerks may be seen wearing masks and monstrous visages at the hours of office. They dance in the choir dressed as women, panders or minstrels. They sing wanton songs. They eat black-puddings at the steps of the altar whilst the celebrant is saying mass. They play at dice there. They cense with stinking smoke from the soles of old shoes. They run and leap through the church without a blush at their own shame. Finally they drive about the town and its theatres in shabby traps and carts; and rouse the laughter of their fellows and the bystanders with infamous performances, with indecent gestures and verses scurrilous and unchaste.' Transvetism was a universal feature of this debauch, which, if one remembers that circumcision is a vestigial form of castration, is not surprising.

In some towns the priests pelted the crowd with black-pudding or rather, in the French original, *boudin*. This word can also mean excrement and this circumstance, if one examines the above quotation, gives one to think. (The Roman fertility festivals sometimes included the throwing of ordure.)

It is particularly interesting to note that the Faculty followed this description with 'a refutation of the argument that such ludi are but the relaxation of the bent bow in a fashion sanctioned by antiquity—on the contrary they are due to original sin and the snares of devils.'

A counter-petition was in turn addressed to the Faculty, asking for the retention of the Feast of Fools: 'We do this according to ancient custom, in order that folly, which is second nature to man and seems to be inborn, may at least once a year have free outlet. Wine casks would burst if we failed sometimes to remove the bung and let in the air. Now we are ill-bound casks and barrels which would let out the wine of wisdom if by constant devotion and fear of God we allowed it to ferment.'

The wearing of masks seems to have been the feature of the

ceremony which was most common and which most enraged the authorities. Riding on a donkey in one form or another seems also to have been a common feature. John Huss describes a Bohemian Feast of Fools:

A clerk, ludicrously attired, was made 'bishop', sat on a donkey facing the tail, and was led to mass in the church. He was fed broth and beer and a rowdy party followed. Torches were carried instead of candles, the priests turned their garments inside out (a simple 'reversal' of their everyday behaviour) and danced. The donkey custom theoretically had its origin in the story of the flight into Egypt.

All efforts to suppress the Feast proved abysmally ineffectual and it continued into the seventeenth century. All that could be done was to attempt to temper it down a little, and in 1444 we find the Chapter of Sens plaintively ordaining that not more than *three* buckets of water are to be poured over the Precentor Stultorum at Vespers, and that those wishing to copulate should please do so outside the church.

The Feast of Fools was a ceremony confined in its celebration to members of the clergy. In the reign of Elizabeth it was finally suppressed, only to be replaced by a secular festival; the election of an 'Abbot of Unreason' or 'Lord of Misrule'.

Stubbes has thus described it:

'Firste, all the wilde heades of the Parish, conventyng together, chuse them a Graund Capitaine (of all mischeef) whom thei innoble with the title of my Lorde of Misserule, and him thei crowne with great solemnitie, and adopt for their kyng.'

The Lord of Misrule then chooses his companions. '. . . twentie, fourtie, three score or a hundred lustie Guttes like to hymself.' These are dressed in his 'livery' . . . 'of Greene, Yellowe, or some other light wanton colour. And as though that were not gaudie (baudie) enough I should saie, thei bedecke themselves with Scarffes, Ribbons and Laces, hanged all over with Golde Rynges, precious stones and other Jewelles: this doen, thei tye about either legge twentie or fourtie belles,

96

with rich hande kercheefes in their handes, sometimes laied a crosse over their shoulders and neckes, borrowed for the moste parte of their pretie Mopsies, and loovyng Bessies, for bussying them in the darcke: Thus all thynges sette in order, then have thei their Hobbie horses, Dragõs and other Antiques, together with their baudie Pipers and Thunderyng Drommes to strike up the Devilles Daunce with all, then marche these Heathen companie towardes the Churche and Churche Yarde, their Pipers pipyng, their Drommers thonderyng, their stumppes Dauncying, their belles tynglyng, their handkerchefes swyngyng about their heades like madmen, their Hobbie horses, and other monsters skirmishyng amongst the throng: and in this sorte thei goe to the churche (though the Minister bee at Praier or Preachyng').

Inside the church they behave like devils incarnate, making such a hullabaloo that nobody can hear himself speak or think. Meanwhile the congregation '. . . the foolishe people thei looke, thei stare, thei laugh, and mount upon formes and pewes to see these goodly pageauntes solemnized in this sorte.'

The Lord of Misrule and his followers then leave the church, and after capering round the building once or twice, settle down to camp in the churchyard where they have previously erected 'their Sommer haules, their Bowers, Arbours and banquettyng houses' and there they 'feaste, banquet and daunce all that daie, and (peradventure) all that night too.' Members of the court of the Lord of Misrule have badges, and these the attendants sell to anybody who will 'maintaine them in this their Heathenrie, Divelrie, Whoredome, Dronkennesse, Pride and what not.' Anyone who refuses to play up to them is 'mocked, and flouted at shamefully.'

Stubbes, who has here inadvertently succeeded, not for the only time, in painting rather an attractive picture of the ceremony he wishes to attack, follows up his description with a stern puritanical warning. Those who give any support to these frolics '. . . fight under the banner and standerd of the Devill, againste Christe Jesus and all his lawes' and, indeed, although the ceremony takes place on consecrated ground, it is perfectly clear that this circumstance is due rather to hostility conscious or unconscious, temporary or permanent, towards the Church than to any feeling that it is some kind of Christian festival.

Later, the Puritans certainly held this view. Prynne, quoting Polydor Vergil, says that the Lords of Misrule are 'derived from the Roman Saturnalia and Bacchanalian festivals; which should cause all pious Christians eternally to abominate them.'

In France also the Feast of Fools declined and vanished, being replaced, as in England, by a *Société Joyeuse*, which was presided over by a *Prince des Sots*, *Mère Folle* or *Abbé de Malgouverne*. Petit de Julleville says, '*La Société Joyeuse c'est la Fête des Fous secularisée.*' The society of Dijon was particularly famous, and it was Philip of Burgundy who, when the Feast of Fools was under fire in the fifteenth century, had authorized its performance by the clergy attached to his palace chapel at Dijon.

The *Mère Folle* was, significantly enough, a man dressed up as woman. Sometimes she took it upon herself to punish a offenders against the society's own peculiar code of morality, usually in the form of wife-beaters. Occasionally she extended her unorthodoxy into political, as well as moral spheres; and in 1603 Louis XIII suppressed the society on account of the disorders which it had caused.

Many of the pagan religions were connected, or perhaps became mixed up with witchcraft, and this connexion is demonstrated by factors in the worship of such deities as Cernunnos, the Horned God, an altar to whom was unearthed beneath the foundations of Notre Dame. Witches of the medieval pattern were probably first invented by the Christian Church in order to explain the erotic phenomena already described, thus providing the pattern for those who felt the urge to express their lack of concord with the sexual attitude of the Church. Many of the stories in connexion with witchcraft—confessions of having sexual intercourse with the devil, etc.—

belong to the realm of sexual fantasy along with the incubi and succubi, and a large proportion of the 'experiences' of those who dabbled in the black arts belong to this category also, the condition being in some instances due to drugs. (It was said, for example, that the witches applied an ointment to their bodies enabling them to fly through the air. The formula of this ointment is known, has been analysed and found to contain atropine and belladonna. These drugs can both induce hallucinations, flying being a stock dream symbol for sexual intercourse.) All the same, actual worship did take place.

The term witchcraft, applied to the activities of certain groups in Europe up to the mid-seventeenth century, is a confusing one, as it embraces four related but definitely distinct phenomena.

Firstly there was the worship of the Horned God in various forms (e.g. Cernunnos) dealt with at length by Margaret Murray. This was essentially the worship of a pagan deity, but in the minds of the Christians who, like most people with immature minds, were excessively prone to the psychological process known as decomposition, there arose a confusion with Christian devils. Secondly, there was a mass of superstitious dread with its source in hysteria and the erotic hallucinations, which became incorporated in the 'evidence' and accusations preferred at witch-trials, confusing the issue, and probably being responsible in part for, thirdly, actual maleficium. Fourthly, inexplicable diseases and disasters which, ironically enough, would now be described as 'acts of God' were attributed to 'the witches'.

The worship of the Horned God was, there is every reason to suppose, a duplication of the Priapeia, Liberalia and Dionysia of ancient Greece and Rome, although probably it resembled the Roman pattern more closely than the Greek. These occasions were accompanied by dancing, a ceremonial feast, and much promiscuous copulation. The arriving witches gave the head of the coven the obscene kiss—a kiss on the buttocks. or on a mask tied to the buttocks. They could be required on initiation to kiss him on any portion of the body that he might require. The female members of the coven had a duty to have intercourse with the devil-deity, or rather with the leader of the coven, whenever he required it, something in the manner of the *jus primae noctis*. Almost certainly he was provided with an artificial phallus for this purpose. The confessions of witches concerning their copulation with the devil frequently included a description of his member, which was described as being 'half as long as a violin', 'covered with scales like a fish', 'like that of a mule', 'ice-cold', 'boiling hot'. Some said he always kept it hanging out of his trousers, others that it was made of horn —'that is why he makes the woman scream so'. Certainly all the women seemed to agree on the pain caused them and only a metal phallus can explain the constant references to the freezing coldness of the devil's penis.

The worshippers of the Horned God were not, in fact, practitioners of witchcraft, i.e. of maleficium.

The dancing mentioned above was an important part of the ceremony, usually taking place in the churchyard. In 1282, the priest of Inverkeithing led the ring in his own churchyard.

Dancing has always been obnoxious to the leaders of a restrictive movement, and the reason for this is not hard to seek. There is, first, the element of spontaneity; and, secondly, the associations with the Theolepsy of the deities of the Ancient World. Dancing releases the emotions, human beings become automatons acting at the dictation of these emotions, and who knows what the nature of these may not be.

Philip Stubbes, who, although he wrote in the sixteenth century, belongs, as a personality, rather to the mid-seventeenth, has much to say on the subject. Besides his own observations, he quotes the views of others—Bullenger: 'Dauncyng, the roote of all filthinesse and uncleannesse.' Calvin: 'Dauncyng, the cheefe mischeefe of all mischeefes'—adding as his own opinion the view that 'dauncers are mad men' that 'Dauncyng stirreth up lust' and that it is 'Vnpossible that daucyng should bee good.'

What applies to the Puritan restrictionists applies likewise to the Medieval. The volume of condemnations of, and prohibitions against dancing was enormous. Dancing occurred, as we have seen, in connexion with witchcraft, the Feast of Fools, and similar ceremonies, and the Church had constantly to be on its guard against infiltration into the form of regular church services. It also appeared in another form. In 1374, in the Low Countries and in Germany, there was a fantastic outbreak of 'Choreomania'. The victims, apparently as the result of physical torture applied in some magical way by the Devil, but presumably also owing to some inner corruptness of the soul, danced frenziedly and unstoppably. They implored their friends to bind their stomachs tightly with rags and bandages, 'otherwise,' they said, 'we shall die.' They displayed also a fanatical fear and dislike of the colour red.

According to Backman, 'They probably appeared more or less naked—this would seem to explain de Herenthal's statement that in their dance they observed no modesty in the presence of spectators; de Mezeray describes them as "stark mad."

'The Choreomaniacs,' he adds, 'are accused by nearly all the chroniclers, as also in the lampoons, of having lapsed into immorality.'

This account suggests that the choreomaniac diabolic possession is perhaps allied to the visits of the incubi and succubi. There is probably also a connexion with flagellantism, for the epidemic, like the epidemic of flagellomania, followed the outbreak of the Black Death.

The Christians sensed the true origin of these phenomena, and the choreomaniacs were accused of both sexual immorality and heresy.

This lumping together by an authoritarian body of all the heresies—religious, sexual and political—the assumption that if a man is guilty of one, he must also be guilty of the others, is of particular interest when one thinks of the tendency of some Americans (and others) during the recent communist witch-hunts in the United States, to suggest that the political default of the offenders was, in some obscure way, connected with homosexual tendencies; and that a homosexual (quite apart from his liability to blackmail) is more liable to turn communist than a heterosexual, and is, accordingly, a greater 'security risk.'

One should be on one's guard, nevertheless, against over-emphasizing the purely 'automatic' part played by the propaganda programme of the Church in causing such outbreaks. Much of it was much more conscious revolt.

The struggle of the Christian Church against dancing had begun as early as the fourth century, although probably at this period it was directed chiefly or entirely against those dances which were openly obscene. St. Augustine would have liked to have prohibited and condemned every form of dance, but he was defeated by quotations from the gospels of St. Matthew and St. Luke (which did not prevent medieval clerics from pretending that the Bible condemned all dancing). The prohibitions multiplied, and increased in severity—in 826 the Council of Rome complained that: 'women, especially on holidays and anniversaries of Saints, only came to church in order to sing shameless songs and to perform choir dances.' As we advance into the Middle Ages a greater and greater number of the prohibitions connect dancing with the Feast of Fools, or the excesses of the flagellants.

Some of those indulging in the illicit dances were certainly acting from unconscious motives like the flagellants and the sufferers from incubi—but others just as certainly were not. To return to the priest of Inverkeithing—an equally serious menace to the Church was the way in which pagan sexuality infiltrated by stealth into the Christian framework. 'Phallic saints' arose, such as St. Foutin (derived from an ingenius transformation of Pothin, the first, and perfectly respectable, Bishop of Lyons), and the Virgin Mary was and is in constant danger of becoming a fertility goddess. This feature of Medieval History, although doubtless worrying enough and irritating enough to the Christian hierarchs, is, to my mind, infinitely reassuring. A small body of neurotic despots attempted to impose an intolerable state of affairs on a previously healthy society, and they failed. They never got a hold on the people they were trying to lead, although God knows, they caused enough harm trying. Even among their own priesthood there were deserters, and it is interesting to see the slender excuses on which the pastor and flock could lapse again into licentiousness.

Moreover a bigger change in moral outlook was in the wind. Medieval man regarded the universe and the men whom it contained as part of an elaborate and interdependent system erected by God. To misbehave was dangerous as well as immoral, for who knew what earthquakes, comets and undesirable cataclysms might not follow. Gradually there dawned in the minds of those who accepted this view of life, the suspicion that it was unjustified, and with this realization came the removal of many restrictions. Like children presented with a nursery-full of new toys they set out to make use of this discovery. It is true, of course, that complete licence is no more satisfying than complete frustration, and that this was a discovery which Renaissance man had still to make. None the less, it was a change, and for that reason, even if for no other, a change for the better. Unfortunately, one thing that did not change was the amount of torture perpetrated daily. It was inflicted by individuals, not by the Church, that was the only difference, or was it? The cruelty of the Church and State had been obsessional cruelty, sometimes sadism for the love of it, and always accompanied by elaborate moral justifications. The Renaissance outlook was very different. Medieval man had been almost entirely preoccupied with and dominated by, the contents of his subconscious. Renaissance man attempted to ignore the existence of his altogether, to divorce himself from it—there were no rules, if you wanted something you went ahead and got it. Cruelty and murder for their own sakes were not a feature of the period—there was always the excuse of money or of lust, but that excuse might be very slender indeed, and crime, when it was committed, was committed without conscience. The Renaissance period can be interpreted as a return to matrism in revolt against a long period of domination by patristic organization and ideas, but in fact it represents much more a failure to identify with anything or anybody at all. It is the age of disassociation, of uninvolvement. Certainly various symptoms of a matrist period are to be observed. The courtesan reappears for the first time since the days of ancient Greece, dress becomes more and more luxurious and voluptuous . . . the *espoitrinement à la façon de Venise* in which rouge was applied to the naked breast as well as to the cheeks. The rich and fashionable developed a passion for scent, and not only human beings but articles of furniture, money and mules were drenched with it. The people, being no longer required to expend vast quantities of energy in suppressing their sexual desires, were able to direct it to other purposes, such as the creation of works of art. Nevertheless the ugly side of the picture remained. . . . The ubiquity of conscienceless, but always rationally motivated violence. One finds this characteristic all down the social scale. Such a one was Sigismondo Malatesta of whom Burckhardt writes: 'It is not only the court of Rome but the verdict of history which convicts him of murder, rape, adultery, incest, sacrilege, perjury and treason, committed not once but often.' To this already impressive list Malatesta would have added an indecent assault on his own son, had not the latter defended himself at the point of a dagger.

Werner von Usslingen had inscribed on his hauberk: 'The Enemy of God, of Pity and of Mercy.'

On 12 August, 1495, the priest Don Niccolo de Pelagati of Figarolo, was shut up in an iron cage outside the tower of San Giuliano at Ferrara. He had twice celebrated his first mass. The first time he had the same day committed murder, but afterwards received absolution at Rome; he then killed four people and married two wives, with whom he travelled about. He afterwards took part in many assassinations, violated women, carried others away by force, plundered far and wide, and infested the territory of Ferrara with a band of followers in uniform extorting food and shelter by every sort of violence.

What applied to the general advancement of personal gain and well-being applied also to sexual adventures.

Sexual 'immorality' extended even into the nunneries . . . in 1497 the Doge of Venice declared that they were 'brothels and houses of assignment' but this did not prevent some young nobles from breaking into a nunnery with the purpose of raping the nuns, and in 1509, in the convent of the Celestia, a number of young patricians took part in a ball and danced all night to the sound of trumpets and fifes. When the Patriarch made a surprise visit to the same institution, he saw a young nun without a veil and with her hair in ringlets. This made him extremely angry, but the other nuns prevented him carrying her off to prison as he wished.

In 1561, the priest Pietro Leon of Valcamonica was: 'living in abominable sin with the nuns committed to his care, who numbered about four hundred, and who for the greater part were young and beautiful. Inside the convent walls he laid aside the mask of hypocrisy and showed himself in his true colours as a lecherous tyrant. He made use of the confessional to seduce the nuns, and, if he met with resistance, he had recourse to imprisonment and torture. In summer he made the fairest of the sisters strip and bathe in the boat-house while he played the role of the elders in the story of Susanna. . . . His table was loaded with pheasants and partridges and excellent wines, and his room was full of comfits and cordials.' Finally: 'some of the nuns, being able to stand it no longer, fled, and denounced the enormities of the priest.'

It will, I hope, be clear by now, that the morals of the age were not really compatible with Christian belief. The Christian Church is an authoritarian Church, and the Renaissance was not a period when authority was respected. Atheist Popes did not conduce to a pious flock. Leo X said, apropos the existence or non-existence of an afterlife: '*Redit in nihilum, quod ante fuit nihil*' and the court of Pope Alexander VI was the scene of a degree of debauchery scarcely creditable, and rejected by some, in whose opinion one would be compelled to join were it not for the (corroborated) evidence of John Burchard, Pontifical Master of Ceremonies and Bishop of Orta and Civita Castellana, the reliability of whose diary must be treated as absolute.

Alexander, born Rodrigo Borja, and father of Cesare and Lucrezia, had early given evidence of his proclivities. In a letter addressed to him by Pius II, that Pope deplores reports of Rodrigo's behaviour which have come to his ears. The letter is dated 11 June, 1460.

'Dear Son,

We have heard that Your Worthiness, forgetful of the high office with which you are invested, was present from the seventeenth to the twenty-second hour, four days ago, in the gardens of Giovanni de Bichis, where there were several women of Siena, women wholly given over to worldly vanities. . . . We have heard that the dance was indulged in with all wantonness; none of the allurements of love were lacking, and you conducted yourself in a wholly worldly manner. Shame forbids mention of all that took place, for not only the things themselves, but their very names are unworthy of your rank. In order that your lust might be all the more unrestrained, the husbands, fathers, brothers and kinsmen of the young women and girls were not invited to be present. You and a few servants were the leaders and inspirers of this orgy.'

This letter apparently had very little effect for, forty-one years later, we read the following report in the diary of Burchard:

'On the evening of 30th October 1501 there was a feast in the rooms of the Duke of Valentinois (Cesare Borgia) in the Papal Palace. Fifty prostitutes of the kind known as courtesans (*corteggiane*) and who are not of the common people, were present. After the meal they danced with the servants and the others who were present. At first they wore their dresses, then they stripped themselves completely naked. The meal over, the lighted candles, which were on the table, were set out on the floor, and chestnuts were thrown down for the naked courtesans to pick up, crawling on hands and knees between the candlesticks. The Pope, the Duke, and Lucrezia his sister were present watching. Finally a collection of silk cloaks, of hose, of brooches, and of other things was displayed, and these were promised to those who had connexion with the greatest number of prostitutes. This took place in public. The spectators, who acted as judges, gave the prizes to those who were adjudged to be the victors.'

Less than a fortnight later, another amusement was arranged for His Holiness. 'A peasant came into the town leading two mares laden with wood. When these animals arrived in St. Peter's Square some of the Pope's servants ran up and caught the harnesses, threw off the packs, and led the mares into the little courtyard which is inside the palace near the gate. Then four stallions belonging to the Palace were released, having neither bridle nor halter. These ran towards the mares and after fighting with teeth and hooves and emitting loud whinnies, they mounted the mares hacking them and wounding them severely. The Pope was at the window of his room situated over the gate of the Palace, and Lucrezia was with him. Both of them watched the spectacle laughing fit to bust, and with evident enjoyment.' (*Cum magno risu et delectatione praedicta videntibus.*)

On Christmas Day, 1503, before the same Pope, an indecent masque was performed. Thirty masquers met on St. Peter's Square. . . . 'There were a great many large false noses shaped like Priapi,' that is having the form of erect penises. 'These, and others, some mounted on donkeys so small that the legs of the riders touched the ground, proceeded to the Palace where the Pope watched them from a window.'

In a letter to Silvio Savelli, Burchard writes of 'rapes, incestuous acts committed in the Palace of St. Peter, infamous things inflicted on adolescents and on young girls, the register of prostitutes admitted to the Palace' and 'children of the Pope born in incest.' Nor was the Pontiff always obliged to pay for his pleasure for at Piombino he 'compelled all the beautiful women and young girls of the town to dance for several hours in the public square in front of his palace.'

This attitude, as has been stated, led to a return to paganism, semi—if not total. Apart from a general lack of 'Christian morals' frequently accompanied by actual atheism, the rule of the Popes was marked by more suggestive incidents. In the reign of Leo X a bull was sacrificed with unmistakably pagan rites in the Forum itself. Lent was marked by an extravagant festival similar to the Roman Saturnalia, described below by Anthony Munday.

'During the time of Shrovetide, there is in Rome a verie great coyle, which they use to call the Carne-vale which endureth the space of three or foure days; all which time the Pope keepeth himself out of Rome, so great is the noyse and hurlie-burlie. The gentlemen will attyre themselves in diverse formes of apparell, some like women, others like Turkes, and everyone almoste in a contrarie order of disguising. And either they be on horsebacke, or in coaches, none of them on foote: for the people that stand on the ground to see this pastime are in very great daunger of their lives, by reason of the running of coaches and great horsses as never in all my life did I see the like stirre.

'And all this is done where the courtizanes be to shew them delight and pastime: for they have coverlettes laid out at their windows, whereon they stand leaning forth, to receive divers devises of rosewater and sweet odours in their faces, which the gentlemen will throw uppe to their windows.

'During this time everye one weareth a disguised visor on his face so that no one knowes what or whence they be; and if anyone bear a secrete malice to an other, he may then kill him, and no body will lay hands on him: for all this time they will obey no lawe. I saw a brave Romaine, who roade there very pleasaunt in his coatch, and suddenly came one who discharged a pistoll upon him; yet no body made any accoumpt, either of the murtherer, or of the slaine gentleman. Besides, there were divers slaine, both by villainy and the horses or the coatches, yet they continued on their pastime making no regard of them.'

The Carnival, like the Feast of Fools was a point where Christian and pagan festivals overlapped, a perpetual and unquenchable danger-spot for the Church. Under Julius III there were extensive bull-baitings in the Forum, Sixtus V made vigorous attempts to suppress it (the Carnival) setting up gibbets in conspicuous places as a warning to the wayward. Any success he may have had was soon forgotten, Florence was particularly renowned for the licentiousness of its Carnival. The festival appears in the United States of America today as the Mardi Gras (q.v.). As in all festivals of this kind, the May Games, Fasching, etc., promiscuous sexual activity played its part.

So far, what has been said, applies, in the main, to Italy. In England the position was different. The Reformation, which was, properly speaking, a reaction to the Renaissance, occurred simultaneously, and, in any case, the Renaissance did not reach England until the time of Henry Tudor. The fact that the Reformation started so early is attributable to factors in the private life of Henry VIII but that is neither here nor there. If it had not been started, indirectly, by the satyriasis of Henry VIII it would have been started later by something else. The point that should be made is that the start was an artificial one, and it is ironical that the beginning of the restrictive movement should have been produced by a venereal disease. For some time the would-be puritan reformers were a minority group, and they will be considered separately in another chapter.

In England, the Renaissance was never accompanied by

the complete failure to form a super-ego that we have seen in Italy. It was rather, a period of balance, a good period from the point of view of those living in it but one not rich in exotic forms of sexual behaviour. It was an age of frankness about sexual matters—textbooks such as the *Quinze Joies de Mariage* and *L'Escole des Filles* were published for the first time.

Even in its modified form the English Renaissance was sufficiently powerful to provoke condemnatory diatribes from the pens of the Puritans. The medieval doctrine that all pleasure is wicked having faded away, the marriage cermony becomes considerably more uninhibited and less concerned with the purely spiritual significance of the union.

Bullenger, in his *The Christian State of Matrimonye*, complains of this:

'Early in the morning the wedded people begynne to exceade in superfluous eating and drinking whereof they spytte until the halfe sermon be done. And when they come to the preaching they are halfe dronke. Some alltogether, therefore, regard they nether the preaching ner prayer but stonde ther only because of the custome.'

And at the celebration after the banquet, when the bride is brought to an open dancing place:

'Then there is such a renninge, leapinge and flynginge amongst them, then there is such a lyftinge up and discouering of damesels clothes and of other wemens apparell that a man might think all these dauncers had cast all shame behinde them and were become starke madde and out of their wyttes and that they were sworn to the deuels daunce. . . . And that noyse and rombling endureth euen until supper.'

And after supper, when the exhausted couple attempt to retire to bed:

'unmannerly and restless people . . . will first go to theyre chambre dore and there syng vicious and naughtie balates that the deuell may haue his tryumphe to the vttermost.'

The Easter fertility festivals, the harvest festivals and the solar festivals at Christmas, which continued underground during the Middle Ages now came out into the open, likewise attracting the scandalized objections of the puritans.

These festivals had considerable interest for the participants, and this was something different from an antiquarian's interest in folklore. This can be clearly seen from the description of Stubbes:

'Against Maie, Whitsondaie, or other time, every parishe, towne and village assemble themselves together, both men women and children, olde and yonge . . . they run gadding to the woods and groues, hils and mountaines, where they spend all the night in pleasaunt pastymes, and in the morning they return, bringing home birch bowes and braunches of trees. . . . Their cheafest jewell they bring home from thence is their maie-poole, which they bring home with great veneration. They have twentie, or fortie yoke of oxen, every Oxe hauing a sweete Nosegaie of flowers tyed on the tippe of his hornes and these Oxen drawe homes this Maiepool (this stinckyng Idoll rather) which is covered all over with Flowers and Hearbes . . . and some time painted with variable colours, with twoo or three hundred Mē and women and children following it, with great deuotion. And thus being reared up with handkercheifs and flagges streamyng on the toppe, they . . . sett up somme haules bowles and arbours hard by it. Then fall they to banquet and feaste, to leape and daunce about it, as ye Heathen people did at the dedication of their Idolles, whereof this is a perfect pattern, or rather the thyng itself.'

The nature of the 'pleasaunt pastymes' is left in no doubt by the observation that, when they return, two-thirds of the girls have been 'defiled'.

The moderation of the English Renaissance, in comparison with the rest of Europe, resulted in a certain amount of criticism of the nasty debauched foreigners, not always offered in a spirit of realism.

William Lithgow, who wrote and travelled in the reign of King James I, condemned with disgust evidences of homo-sexual behaviour which he encountered during his perigrinations of Europe. In Padua; which he considered 'the most melancholy city in Europe' . . . 'the schollers . . . in the night commit many murthers against their privat adverseries, and too often executed upon the stranger and the innocent: for beastly sodomy, it is rife here as in Rome, Naples, Florence, Bullogna, Venice, Ferrara, Genoa, Parma not being exempted, nor yet the smallest village of Italy; a monstrous filthinesse, and yet to them a pleasant pastime, making songs and singing sonets of the beauty and pleasure of their Bardassi, or buggerd boyes.'

But the Reformation, which had begun early in England, was spreading to other parts of Europe. Unfortunately the reaction against the Christian prohibitions had been too strong . . . the harder the pendulum is swung the faster it returns, the excesses of the Renaissance had proved too much, and, instead of choosing a vertical position, it was back, or almost, in the position whence it started.

FOUR

PURITAN AND RAKE

In England, as has been said, a period of overlap existed, during which restrictive and sexually anarchic tendencies existed for a time side by side.

One of the most dangerous features of those who seek to exercise authority of the sort practised by the Puritan fathers, and the fathers of the Medieval Church is that the very nature, the very core and essence of the unpleasantness of their aims lead to the success of these. Those who wish to exercise power can generally do so if they try hard enough, particularly if the men who they seek to dominate are in such a condition of revolt against authority as to be unable to endure enough organization to oppose them successfully. The entire energy of the would-be patriarch is diverted to his aims. The tolerant, anarchic and sexually uninhibited man disposes of his through a variety of channels.

Of all the various branches and sects of the Puritan movement, none so clearly exemplifies the character of the rest as Calvanism. This creed placed stress above all else on the sanctity of authority—and in particular of paternal authority. In Scotland a child was decapitated for striking its father. The Calvinists had the passion of the mentally immature for written rules and regulations. Special penalties were prescribed for every offence which their neurosis-ridden minds could conceive. For criticizing Calvin's doctrines Gruet (who wrote 'nonsense' in the margin of one of the master's books) was detected; and executed for blasphemy and treason, the union of Church and State making one offence both. To address Calvin as 'Calvin' instead of as 'Mr. Calvin' incurred an almost equally severe penalty. Women were mentally returned to a position of inferiority, admiration of the Virgin Mary was, of course, taboo, and the idea of women occupying positions of authority anathema. Knox wrote his pamphlet, 'The First Blast of the Trumpet against the Monstrous Regiment of Women', which he unluckily timed to coincide with the accession of Queen Elizabeth I, extricating himself from this predicament as best he could in a long correspondence with Somerset.

But the Puritan authority was not quite like that of the Medieval Church. Like the Medievals, the Puritans tried to incubate guilt in the minds of their flock, but, in the first place they had widened their field of fire, and were concerned not with sexual guilt alone but with guilt of every kind, and, in the second, unlike the Medievals, they did not succeed.

The battery of propaganda, even if ineffective, was noisy, continuous and unrestrained. Calvin asks: 'do not our innumerable and daily transgressions deserve more severe and grievous chastisements than those which His clemency inflicts on us? Is it not highly reasonable that our flesh should be subdued, and, as it were, accustomed to the yoke, lest it should break out, according to its propensities, with lawless excesses?' Here we see an important aspect of the whole restrictive movement, a dread of spontaneity, a fear of what will be released if 'authority' were not maintained . . . 'the licentiousness of the flesh which, unless it be rigidly restrained transgresses every bound,' and the same idea is to be found elsewhere: pleasure is proportional to the degree to which mental control is relaxed. In this lies the explanation of the 'disassociation' of the Renaissance and Restoration.

In another aspect the Puritan authority differed from the Medieval. Its rule was, like the Medieval, the rule of a father over his family, but with this notion went one not present in the earlier situation. The Puritan Church abandoned the idea that virginity was good (except of course in the case of the unmarried); it stressed, on the contrary, the importance of having a large family, and seemed almost on the point of restoring polygamy. Knox himself, whilst opposed to 'regimented' women, appeared to have no objection to being followed about by an adoring flock of them. He married twice, caused some scandalous talk by the closeness of his relationship with a Mrs. Bowes, suddenly married her daughter and withdrew with both of them to Geneva, ignoring the outraged protests of Mr. Bowes. Knox then added to his collection a Mrs. Locke, *her* daughter and her maid. On the Sabbath he proceeded to church in state, followed (at a suitable distance) by his five women, who were soon made six by the addition of a Mrs. Adamson. It is improbable that these relationships, other than that with Mrs. Knox, were, in the usual sense, sexual ones. The Puritan fear of spontaneity already mentioned was a deep-seated one.

By means of a kind of police-state the lives of the citizens could be interfered with in all kinds of intolerable ways. Apart from the suppression of every kind of activity savouring of the dreaded relaxation of mental control . . . dancing, drinking, singing, the may-pole, and the celebration of Easter and Christmas; measures were taken to ensure the prevalence of positive gloom. Attendance at church was compulsory on Wednesdays and Sundays, and police were used to enforce this regulation, but people who went to church at other times were punished. Bridesmaids were arrested for decorating a bride too gaily, and men and women punished for eating fish on Fridays, dressing in cheerful clothes and making jokes. Swearing was, it need hardly be said, a serious offence, the Puritans objecting not only to blasphemy and the use of sexual obscenities, but extending their dislike to all words connected with the excrementary functions.

Those who so much as showed their resentment at the ordainments of the fathers did so at their peril. The parents of a child who objected when the priest christened it by a name other than that which they themselves had requested, being arrested on the spot for, as usual, treason and blasphemy.

One of the most significant forms of propaganda and regulation were those concerning dress. The Puritans attempted, for reasons which should not be too obscure, to masculinize men as far as possible, and correspondingly, to de-feminize and make negative, members of the opposite sex. In 1654 Thomas Hall published his pamphlet: 'The Loathsomnesse of Long Haire . . . with an appendix against Painting, Spots, Naked Breasts, etc.' Opening with a selection of repetitive and long-winded verse:

> How many doe I daily see
> Given up to Muliebritie
> A female head to a male face
> Is marryed now in every place.

and much more in the same vein. The Bible has been gutted of useful quotations, a study of these resulting in the conclusion that it is just as much a sin totally to shave the head as it is to wear the hair too long. This gave rise to the difficult question: 'How long that haire is which the scripture condemns?' Throughout the treatise it is emphasized that what is wrong about long hair is that it is not merely a sign of vanity but *womanly* as well, all kinds of contortionist arguments being employed to prove that Nature intended men to wear their hair 'poll'd'.

His address to women is phrased more as a plea than as a harangue, women being implored not deliberately to arouse lust in the hearts of men.

Make-up is 'the badge of an harlot, rotten posts are painted, and gilded nutmegs are usually the worst.' Dyeing the hair is wicked because it makes a fool of St. Matthew, who says, v. 36: 'No man can make one haire white or black.' And as for the 'Naked Breasts'! They are 'temptations and known provocations to uncleanliness. . . . Pious matrons are modest: it is only light ones, and such as are for sale, that thus invite customers by setting open shop windows.'

To enforce their disgusting regulations, all the puritan sects, and, in particular, Calvin, resorted to violence, torture and execution. The outlets available to the Medieval sufferers were not available to their seventeenth-century counterparts simply because the Puritans were more ruthless in enforcing their desires. Believing with all their hearts that the end justifies the means, and unable to achieve their ends by propaganda alone, they had at their disposal more efficient means of organization, and with a gauleiter in every village they were able to be more ruthless. Popular feeling as everybody knows was against these extremes, this being adequately demonstrated by the fact that the Puritans found it necessary to make use of such violent methods.

Perhaps the second sentence of the preceding paragraph requires qualification. In 1641 a pamphlet was published, attacking the activities of a sect known as the Family of Love, which had been founded in the sixteenth century by Nicolaes.

Susanna Snow, the daughter of a respectable gentleman living at Pitford in Surrey, talking one day to one of her father's men, began to question him about the 'new sects of religion', inquiring what news he had heard of any of them. He told her of a society 'numbering about an hundred' which 'every day had a meeting in a private place, which was mistrusted to be about the sign of the Buck' at Bagshot. The great suspicion was that they were interlopers from London, but 'it was the talk of the whole country.' This information Susanna Snow carefully absorbed, and after a sleepless night, rose before the sun, and gobbling her breakfast rode off 'side-saddle on a gelding . . . so great a desire had this poor gentlewoman to thrust herself into danger.'

When she had arrived on the outskirts of Bagshot, she saw a party of at least a hundred, male and female, crossing the heath. She approached a female straggler, and by means of deceit, pretending she already had a rendezvous, which she had missed, with the Family of Love, elicited the information that this was, indeed, the sect in question. Thus she obtained admission to the society.

The Family had 'certain days, which are dedicated unto

saints, as they call them.' The saints included Ovid . . . 'who wrote the Art of Loving' and Priapus, 'the first bawdy butcher that did ever stick prick in flesh and make it swell.' At their meetings in the woods they were addressed by the leader, who 'began to speak most strong language such as this or the like: "let us not persuade ourselves, although that many would have us believe it, that our great god Cupid is obcecated, for he penetrateth the intrails of the most magnanimous." ' 'After these or the like words, he recited part of a verse from Vergil's Epigrams: *Non stat bené mentula crassa* . . . on this he built his whole discourse, venting very strange obscene passages; after this was done, they go to dinner where they had exceeding delicates.'

During the ceremonies, the leader of the sect had taken such a fancy to Susana, 'that he must either enjoy or perish.' Accordingly, on the way back from the woods he singled her out, and made the following elaborately loquacious pass.

'Fair sister, hard is that task, when I must die in silence, or else present unto you an unseemly suit; but so irksome is death, and so pleasant the enjoyment of my wishes, that I rather desire to be counted unmannerly, than not amorous to your beauteous self.'

This proved successful: and Susanna was taken to the rest of the sisters, among whom she remained for a whole week. She then returned home, explaining her absence by saying she had been staying at her aunt's at Oakingham. Her mother knew this to be untrue, but could get no other answer from her. Miss Snow now became moody, taking to brooding alone in her bedroom, and smashing glasses and crockery, sometimes on the heads of the servants. Her parents, worried to distraction, sent to Oxford for the assistance of a Mr. Ybder, 'a most reverend divine'. No sooner had Mr. Ybder arrived at the house than he was led upstairs by the distraught parents. Benevolently smiling, he entered the room, but 'she shrieked out "the devil, the devil; I am damned, I am damned, I am damned": with many such like horrible exclamations.'

Mr. Ybder assured her she was mistaken, and for a while she consented to listen to him, 'but then she became very troublesome, and sometimes outrageous', calling for glasses of water, and then dashing them to the ground. Finally she was quietened and reassured, but the curious tale was out.

Shades of the middle ages surround this whole business. One is reminded of the Incubus illusions, and also of the habit of the Medieval Church of tarring all their enemies with every kind of brush. Heretics were accused not only of heresy, but of witchcraft, homosexuality, bestiality too. In some of these illusions they were supported by the erotic illusions of the sexually starved and the neurotic; whose condition they themselves had done so much to foster. Was the same process repeated in the seventeenth century? The suspicion that this may have been the case makes it difficult to guess the true nature of the activities and beliefs of the Family of Love. There is no real means of telling, and one person's guess is as good as another s. But whether one treats it in the light of fantasy or of fact, it is a significant example of the result of too intolerable a pressure on those unsuited or unwilling to stand the strain.

The Roman Catholic Church was, naturally enough, eager to check these tendencies. However, they were well enough aware that they would meet with little success if they continued in the same easy-going spirit in which they rolled along so happily during the Renaissance. To check an authoritarian movement one must oneself be authoritarian, and paradoxical though it may seem, the Roman Church developed several of the characteristics of the Church that it was trying to resist. It became extremely authoritarian. The doctrine of Papal Infallibility, in its most violent and unrealistic form, appeared, corresponding to the Puritan passion for rules and regulations drawn, and interpreted according to their own inclination, from the Bible.

The doctrine of Papal Infallibility frequently resulted in embarrassment. Pope Alexander VI, under the mistaken conviction that the earth was flat, drew a line on the map, stating that according to information received, all land to the west of it was Spanish, all to the east Portuguese. The Portuguese promptly circumnavigated the globe in an easterly direction, and landing on the South American continent laid claim to Brazil.

As the Catholics progressed along the same track they became bitten with the same diseases as their enemies. Signs of the same spontaneity phobia, the same dread of scientific or of any other kind of inquiry; of anything inconsistent with a blind devotion to sacred authority, reared their ugly heads, breeding the atmosphere that led to the trial of Galileo, the execution of Giordano Bruno, the torture of Campanella, all accompanied by the revival of a mental attitude of Sadism.

In time, Catholics modified their objection to the euphoric provided the euphoria in question was based on orthodox imagery approved as desirable by the Church.

With the restoration of King Charles II, the actual physical necessity, from motives of self-preservation, of abstaining from illicit sexual relief, was removed. Yet it appears that the English people *as a whole* did not relapse immediately into a state of debauchery. There was of course terrific celebration of the return of the King, some of which took such significant form as the rearing-up of maypoles, the livening up of marriage celebrations and the wearing of colourful clothes, but among those not of the fast' set comprised of members of the aristocracy near the King, there was balance rather than excess. In court circles things were somewhat different. Sexual and alcoholic excess springs in many cases from having too much money and correspondingly little to do. Even during the Tudor period of balance there had been wild sparks, male and female. John Aubrey says of Mary, Countess of Pembroke, the sister of Sir Philip Sidney: 'She was a beautifull ladie and had an excellent witt, and had the best breeding that that age could afford. Shee had a pritty sharpe-ovall face. Her haire was of a reddish-yellowe.

'She was very salacious, and she had a contrivance that in the spring of the yeare, when the stallions were to leap the mares, they were to be brought before such a part of the house where she had a *vidette* to look on them and please herself with their sport: and then she would act the like sport herself with *her* stallions. One of her great gallants was crooke-back't Cecill earl of Salisbury.'

An even more astonishing glimpse of the way in which some members of the aristocracy passed the time in their country houses, is obtained by reading the transcript of the trial of Mervyn, Lord Castlehaven, who on 5 April, 1631, was tried: 'For abetting a Rape upon his Countess, Committing Sodomy with his servants, and Commanding and Countenancing the Debauching of his Daughter.'

Tried before his peers in Westminster Hall, an amazing tale was told by the witnesses, consisting of the earl's servants, his wife and his daughter.

The servants had been compelled to rape Lady Ann, the Countess, and then to sleep with the earl himself. Two of these servants in particular, Antill and Skipworth, were the favourites of the earl, and the last of the two he had married to his daughter.

Lady Audley, junior, stated in her evidence that: 'I was first persuaded to lie with Skipwith by the Earl's persuasion and Threatenings, saying I should have nothing but what Skipwith gave me. He saw Skipwith and I lie together several times and so did many Servants of the House besides. . . . He used Oyl to enter my body first, for I was then but Twelve Years of Age and usually lay with me by the Earl's Privity and Command.'

Lady Audley, senior's, evidence was to the effect that: 'The first or second Night after we were Married, Antill came to our Bed, and the Lord Audley talk'd lasciviously to me and told me my body was his, and if I lay with any Man with his consent, 'twas not my fault but his. He made Skipwith come naked into our Chamber and Bed: and took delight in calling up his servants to show their Nudities, and forc'd me to look upon them and to commend those that had the longest. Broadway, a servant of My Lord's, by His Lordship's Command, lay with me, and I making resistance, My Lord Audley held my hands and one of my Feet. . . . He delighted to see the Act done, and made Antill come into the Bed to us and lie with me in such a manner as he might see it, and though I cry'd out, he never regarded the Complaint I made, but incouraged the Ravisher.'

Evidence of various servants followed, all confirming what had been said by the two ladies. Broadway added that after he had raped Lady Castlehaven, the earl: 'used my body as a Woman.' He confirmed also the evidence concerning Skipwith and the young Lady A. . . . 'and when he got upon her Lord Audley stood by, and incouraged him to get her with child, for he would rather have a boy of (Skipwith's) getting than of any other.'

Another servant, Fitzpatrick, said that Skipwith was a great favourite of Lord Audley and 'usually lay in Bed with him'. Fitzpatrick himself had often been to bed with Lord Audley and believed that most of the other servants had done likewise. He also added that Castlehaven 'kept a Woman in his house called Blandina, who was a Common Whore to his Lordship and his Servants. His House was a Common Brothel-House, and the Earl himself took delight not only in being an Actor, but a Spectator while other Men did it. Blandina was once abused by himself and his servants for the space of seven Hours together, until she got the French Pox.'

Castlehaven's defence, that it was true that his servants had lain in bed with him, but that this was only due to temporary shortage of space, and that the whole business was, in any case, a put-up job on the part of his son, who wished to dispose of him in order to obtain possession of the estate, was not well received, and the unfortunate peer was duly decapitated.

The whole amazing situation at the earl's various country houses in Wiltshire can best be explained as an extraordinary retreat from reality, savouring almost of the mystical attitude towards sexual matters of much more primitive peoples, but without the innocence and naïvety of the ancient, into a desperate fantasy world of childish make-believe. Castlehaven may have been actually mentally deranged, it is more likely that his behaviour was an exaggerated example, symptomatic of a state of ennuie affecting several decades.

King Charles himself in honesty can be said to stand out among the members of the court as a man not conforming to the general pattern. He might be almost insatiable in his sexual desires. He might be unscrupulous about the way in which he acquired possession of the women whom he desired, giving short shrift to the dismayed husband. Ugly as sin though he was, he might, when he had obtained possession of these women, discard and change them with kaleidoscopic rapidity. There was another side to him. Athletic, in the summer evenings he would go down to Putney to swim in the river, and in the mornings, whilst everybody else was lying exhausted in bed after the previous night's excesses he would rise with the sun and play two hours' vigorous tennis on the palace court. He transacted a phenomenal quantity of business, he was deceptively astute in political and business activities alike. Interested in everything, he conversed on four successive walks in the palace gardens with Evelyn on Astronomy, Smoke Abatement, Architecture and Gardening, his collection of curiosities, and Bees.

But Charles himself was an exception. Already there were signs of that element of cruelty which began as cruelty of the Renaissance type, but which, by the turn of the century had come to exercise a frightful fascination over those who practised it—a horrid repetition of the Roman situation we have already seen.

At first this began among the court set, and remained among the rest of the population, as a kind of straightforward, healthy, honest-to-God, no-nonsense attitude towards life. People were sick of endless self-control, of being nagged at about the state of their consciences, and, as in the Renaissance period, they disconnected themselves from these organs altogether. At Claydon an old labourer drained the communion cup to the dregs, swearing he would have his money's worth out of it 'being he paid for it.' In London, when effigies of the Pope and Cardinals were burnt amid the cracking of fireworks and howls of execration, they were filled with live cats to make them scream realistically. Men were quick to take offence; a gallant elbowed in the crowd would, as like as not, run the jostler through before thinking twice about it.

One typical figure of the time was Sir Charles Sedley, wit and dramatist, whom Charles II told that 'nature had given him a Patent to be Apollo's viceroy.' He was married to a Roman Catholic girl, who unfortunately soon became unmistakably insane, being fantastically vain and finally insisting on being always addressed as 'Your Majesty.' Sedley's daughter Catherine was, at one time, the favourite mistress of James, Duke of York. Whether, owing to his marital difficulties or as seems more likely, to his innate personal wildness, Sedley soon gained a reputation as the most unbridled of the rakes. Amusing though he was universally admitted to be, there was a streak of spitefulness in him; he had Kynaston beaten up by hired thugs for appearing in a ridiculous parody of his, Sedley's, manner and dress. Some time about the middle of 1663 he was in trouble together with various other sparks for a wild party held in the Cock Tavern in Bow Street. An entry in Pepys' Diary refers to this.

'1st July 1663 . . . after dinner we fell talking, Sir J. Minnes, Mr. Batten and I, Mr. Batten telling us of a late triall of Sir Charles Sydley the other day, before my Lord Chief Justice Foster and the whole bench, for his debauchery a little while since at Oxford Kate's, coming in open day into the Balcone and showing his nakedness . . . and abusing of scripture and as it were from thence preaching a mountebank sermon from the pulpit, saying that there he had to sell such a powder as should make all the (women) in town run after him, and that being done, he took a glass of wine . . . and then drank it off, and then took another and drank the king's health.'

The dots are from the Wheatley edition, the fullest available. The reader may be able to insert some of the missing passages himself.

Dr. Johnson, in his *Lives of the Poets*, gives this version of the same incident. 'Sackville . . . with Sir Charles Sedley and Sir Thomas Ogle, got drunk at the Cock in Bow street, by Covent Garden, and going into the balcony exposed themselves to the populace in very indecent postures. At last, as they grew warmer, Sedley stood forth naked, and harangued the populace in such profane language that the publick indignation was awakened; the crowd attempted to force the door, and being repulsed, drove in the performers with stones, and broke in the windows of the house. For this misdemeanour they were indicted.'

Sedley was fined the considerable sum of two thousand marks, and, says Pepys, 'The Judges did all of them round give him a most high reproof; My Lord Chief Justice saying: That it was for him, and for such wicked wretches as he was, that God's anger and judgement hung over us, calling him Sirrah many times.'

Five years later Sedley was in trouble again, Pepys' Diary for 23 October, 1688, telling us that: 'This day Pierce do tell me, among other news, the late frolick and debauchery of Sir Charles Sidley and Buckhurst, running up and down all the night with their arses bare, through the streets; and at last fighting, and being beat by the watch and clapped up all night.'

Buckhurst, who had been the first man to keep Nell Gwynn (next door to the King's Head Inn at Epsom, where he, Nell and Sedley kept 'merry house', as Pepys learnt when he stayed at the inn), and who having been arrested on more than one occasion (the first time for murder), was almost as wild a fellow as Sedley, but on this occasion the King lent his moral and actual support, having, it seems, been involved in the party himself in the earlier part of the evening. The unfortunate constable who had effected the arrest was 'laid . . . by the heels to answer it next sessions: which is a horrid shame.'

Among his other exploits Sir Charles had a brush with Gilbert Sheldon, Archbishop of Canterbury, after whom the Sheldonian Theatre at Oxford is named. The circumstances, according to the entry in Pepy's Diary for 29 July, 1667, were as follows.

'Among other discourse my cousin Roger told us a thing certain, that the Archbishop of Canterbury, as now is, do keep a wench, and is as very a wencher as can be; and tells us that it is a thing publicly known that Sir Charles Sidley had got away one of the Archbishop's wenches from him, and the Archbishop sent to him to let him know that she was his kinswoman, and did wonder that he would offer any dishonour to one related to him. To which Sir Charles Sidley is said to have answered: "A pox take his Grace! Pray tell his Grace that I believe he finds himself too old, and is afraid that I should out do him among his girls, and spoil his trade." '

What the truth of this incident may be is hard to guess.

Sedley lived to see the beginning of the eighteenth century in which he more properly belonged, but in 1680 was severely concussed by a collapsing tennis-court, after which he appears never to have been quite the same again, turning in his latter years almost towards religious mania.

All the same, this activity in its extremes was confined to the fast court set. The plays of the Restoration are often cited as examples of the general debauchery of the age. At this period the theatre was patronized almost entirely by the upper classes. The playhouses were already, as they became still more in the next century, pick-up places and a setting for coarse badinage.

Charles appears to have tried, although perhaps only spasmodically, to maintain a certain level of dignity in his court, possibly in emulation of Louis XIV. He did his best to keep drunkenness at a low level, and free conduct did not mean free speech, for he expelled Henry Killigrew from the court for saying that Barbara Villiers had been, since her earliest youth, 'a little lecherous girl'. The expulsion is the more, or, if you take the cynical attitude, the less surprising, since the accusation was undoubtedly well-founded. Alone of all Charles's mistresses pure lust appeared sometimes to outweigh political or financial motives in determining her conduct. Before she was fifteen she had formed a liason with Lord Chesterfield, and long after she had come to an arrangement with Charles she continued to sleep around openly and frequently. Her behaviour attracted general public disapproval, part of which was expressed in the publication of an anonymous broadsheet, 'The Poor Whores Petition'.

In spite of his pretended decorum Charles occasionally lapsed into a less artificial attitude towards his mistresses. Evelyn has described something which took place at Arlington's house, Euston, when 'the whole house was filled from end to end with lords, ladies and gallants; there being such a furnished table as I had seldom seen, nor anything more splendid and free.' One suspects that Evelyn, unmitigated old hypocrite that he was, must have known and seen more than he lets on, although the chief motive in telling the following story appears to be the clearing of his own name.

'Oct. '71. It was universally reported that the fair Lady Whore was bedded one of these nights and the stocking flung, after the manner of a married bride. I acknowledge that she was for the most part in her undress all the day and that there was fondness and toying with that young wanton; nay 'twas said, I was at the former ceremony, but 'tis utterly false. I never saw nor heard of any such thing whilst I was there, though I had been in her chamber, and all over that apartment late enough, and was myself observing all passages with much curiosity. However, 'twas confidently believed she was first made a misse as they call these unhappy creatures, with solemnity at this time.'

Sound reason for believing the rumours was provided exactly nine months later by the birth to the fair Lady Whore

—Louise Penancoet de Kéroualle—of a child, generally believed to be Charles's.

The Renaissance type violence and sexual excesses of the Restoration might be confined to a small group and might also be alien to the character of the King himself.

The violence was to prove as infectious and as poisonous as it had to the Roman Empire and the climax of the disease was to prove if possible still less desirable.

FIVE

THE MEDMENHAMITES AND THE GEORGIAN RAKES

THE eighteenth century was an age of clubs. In no other period have men with similar interests shown such a propensity for joining together in a formalized society. This applies just as much to those with disreputable qualities in common as to those with a more serious purpose. During the course of the century there was a definite trend in both kinds of club to become more and more formalized, and to draw up more and more rules and regulations. There was also a tendency within the disreputable body to become more and more respectable, or, at any rate, less and less violent. (This tendency was, of course, reflected throughout the social framework.)

In the early years of the century the Rakes' clubs, of which there were a large number in London, still showed all too plainly their descent from the 'roaring boys' of the previous century. The bucks and gallants roamed the streets terrifying the elderly, beating up the watch, breaking windows, committing rape and sometimes even murder. Young girls were stood on their heads in the gutter, and elderly ladies popped into barrels and sent rolling down Snow Hill. Violence was the order of the day, as witness such clubs as the 'Mohawks' and the 'Man-killers'. The Mohawks terrorized the town for a considerable period. They had invented a pastime which they called 'tipping the lion'. This consisted in crushing the nose, and simultaneously gouging out the eyes of the victims unfortunate enough to be waylaid by them. They also carried a piece of apparatus for distending mouths, and, as an alternative to these occupations sometimes slit the ears of their prisoner. There were certainly several of these clubs in London during the first two or three decades of the century and their activities so far surpassed the description of horse-play that they were gradually driven out of existence. From then onwards the eighteenth-century gallant had to pursue discreet vices.

There were at this time a very large number of brothels, houses of assignment, and dubious taverns in London, and no shortage of prostitutes to fill them. They had the advantage of being well advertised, for 'Harris' List of Covent Garden Ladies' was published annually, ennumerating in detail the physical charms and accomplishments of all the better-known bawds in the locality. (So successful did this enterprise prove, that Harris later published a companion guide to the ladies of Piccadilly.)

The foremost vice of the age was drink, not sexual immorality, but one thing leads to another, and although the great majority of the rakes' clubs never had women present at their meetings, they constantly discussed them, and often finished off the evening's carousal with a visit to a brothel or to a theatre where whores and demireps were to be found in quantity and variety. Ned Ward, journalist-author of *The Secret History of Clubs*, describes a typical evening spent by the members of the Beaus' Club. After becoming fairly drunk on 'Champaigne, Burgundy and Hermettage', they took out their snuff-boxes, and having refreshed their nostrils, proceeded to drink the health of 'some celebrated play-house wanton, Haymarket punk or court curtizan.' The health was succeeded by a long lecture on 'her heaving dumplins, her lushious juicy lips and drowsy leacherous pignies, with all the outward signs that her charming ladyship imparts to signify that she's an indefatigable bedfellow.' Having drunk themselves into a state of adequate courage and enthusiasm with making such toasts they then sally forth to the play, or, more accurately, 'to attack the mask'd ladies who hang about the theatre in their second-hand furbiloes to open the wicket of love's bear garden to any bold sportsman who has a venturesome mind to give a run to his puppy.'

The bawds and strumpets used to frequent the eighteen-penny gallery of the theatres, to which they gained admittance by what means we can only surmise, but which did not, apparently, involve payment in money. Not all of them, how-ever, did their business in theatres. There was founded, *c.* 1670, a club known as 'The Dancing Club'. This consisted chiefly of 'bullies, libertines and strumpets,' says Ward, who is scathing (and amusing) in his description of the members. 'To the membership of this club there was no limit to number or quality, but any person was free to shake their rumps and exercise their members to some tune.' Professional whores, such as Oyster Moll, 'whose crinigerous clift was ready to run the gantlope through a regiment of foot-guards,' attended; and doubtless gave the proceedings a helping hand in the right direction, although, since both sexes seem to have come to the club with the principal object of obtaining sexual gratification ('to put their arses, by one sort of dancing, in tune for another'), it is hardly surprising that the proceedings were a success. Indeed, the dancing-master who started the club soon had to move to more commodious premises. The dancing that took place was wild and Corybantic and not of the kind taught at most dancing schools. The company rapidly reached a condition of frenzy, though not, says Ward, of elegance. They appear to have consisted very largely of servants who had taken the opportunity to borrow some of their masters' and mistresses' clothes, but young gallants used to attend in the hopes, which were likely to be fulfilled, of obtaining the favours of some servant-girl. Ward elaborates at length on the wildness and capering of the dancers, and adds that retiring rooms were provided for the benefit of those seized with the desire to try the other kind of dancing; but some of the company appear to have lacked the financial resources necessary to indulge in this luxury, and to have subsided on the floor amongst the legs of the dancers.

Thus it would seem that many public whores attended more or less private functions, sometimes by invitation, sometimes by intrigue, and on their own initiative. Fancy-dress balls often provided an excuse for inadequate or indecent clothing.

Lady Elizabeth Montague gives a catty description of the costume of a certain Miss Chudleigh at a ball in 1750:

'Miss Chudleigh's dress, or rather, undress, was very interesting. She represented "Iphegenia before her sacrifice" but she was so unclothed that the High Priest had no difficulty at all in closely examining the victim. The ladies, who themselves were not too strait-laced, were so revolted at this that they refused to speak to her.'

Some of the richer degenerates of the age did not deign to find their delights in the public stews. Such men as Colonel Charteris, a thief, a cheat, and a coward, who in 1730 was convicted of committing a rape on his maidservant, and of whom Arbuthnot wrote in the *Gentleman's Magazine* that 'he persisted in spite of age and infirmities in the pursuit of every human vice except prodigality and hypocrisy', who kept a private seraglio at Hornby Castle with an elderly matron to administer it, could afford more secluded pleasures.

William Douglas, or 'Old Q', was reputed to hold infamous orgies at 138 Piccadilly and at his villa in Richmond. Sly allusions were made to his goings-on, his house being referred to as the home of 'oriental voluptuousness' and 'refined sensuality'.

He died as a result of eating too much fruit, managing, by hook or by crook, to keep himself sexually active 'til the end.

Sir Francis Dashwood had a share in Mrs. Stanhope's bawdy-house near Drury Lane, and this doubtless proved useful to him in supplying the wherewithal for his activities at Medmenham and West Wycombe. The absence of sex-life combined with club-life did not disturb the rakes, who could always take a party to a brothel, such as Molly King's, Mother Douglas's, Mrs. Gould's, or even to the house of the famous Mrs. Goadby, who, after a visit to France, made many innovations and refinements in English hetaeric life. Here it was possible to obtain food and drink as well as girls.

If sexual relations with prostitutes can ever be said to be satisfactory, then the eighteenth century was the period when purchased enjoyment was most likely to prove enjoyable. The brothels of eighteenth-century London could be used for private parties, and were equipped and managed in a way which showed that the proprietors, at any rate, took their professional duties seriously.

Mrs. Goadby, mentioned above, drew up strict regulations for the observance of the girls in her employ. Their drinking and eating habits were particularly the subject of control. The customer must be satisfied always and in any way.

Casanova visited England and investigated the hetaeric life of the city. At the end of an evening spent in the company of a male friend and two girls, it was suggested that the company dance the 'Rompaipe' naked. Blindfold musicians were obtained and the doors locked, but Casanova himself would not participate, and was not in fact greatly impressed.

'It was one of those moments when I knew many truths. On that occasion I saw that the pleasures of love are the result, and not the cause of gaiety. I had before my eyes three superb bodies, admirable in their freshness and regularity: their movements, their gestures, even the music, everything was ravishing and seductive, but no emotion came to tell me that I was sensible of it.'

This was clearly a private party. All the better-class brothels were run on the 'salon' system. The clientele assembled in the drawing-room after the theatre.

Charlotte Hayes, who was quick to follow the example of Mrs. Goadby, and to equip her girls with dresses, watches and gold ear-rings, kept a brothel in King's Place, Pall Mall, the visitors to which, says Bloch (*Sexual Life in England*), 'were nearly all impotent debauchees who required every possible stimulation for the satisfaction of their lusts.'

One day Charlotte Hayes sent the following invitation to her clients.

'Mrs. Hayes commends herself respectfully to Lord ——,

and takes the liberty of advising him that this evening at 7 o'clock precisely 12 beautiful nymphs, spotless virgins, will carry out the famous Feast of Venus as it is celebrated in Tahiti, under the instruction and leadership of Queen Oberea (which role will be taken by Mrs. Hayes herself).'

Hawksworth, Cook's travelling companion, had described how in Tahiti 'young men and girls often copulate publicly before the people, receiving good advice from the bystanders, usually women, amongst whom the most important inhabitants are to be found. Thus the girls (of 11 years) receive their information at an early age.'

Mrs. Hayes, having read Hawksworth's account, had decided to carry out the same ceremonies before her guests in King's Place. According to Bloch, twenty-three people responded to the invitation, including five members of the House of Commons.

'Punctually at 7 o'clock the feast began, for which, for the men's parts, Mrs. Hayes had engaged twelve athletic youths. These youths, with the nymphs, now celebrated the Tahiti Venus Feast before the eyes of the entranced audience; after which a sumptuous meal was taken.'

Miss Falkland had a brothel known as 'The Temple of Mysteries', where orgies of an unspeakable and, unfortunately, mysterious, nature were supposed to take place. This lady had two other brothels, one an apprentice establishment known as 'The Temple of Flora' and another—'The Temple of Aurora'.

A more moderate form of sexual enjoyment was provided by the 'posture' girls, who stripped themselves naked and stood on the table in the middle of the room. A girl called 'Posture Nan' was a celebrated mistress of this art.

'Urbanus' in *The Midnight Spy* attacks this custom. The scene is a Great Russell Street brothel.

'Behold an object, which arouses at once our disgust and our pity. A beautiful woman lies stretched on the floor, and offers to the view just those parts of her body that, were she not without all shame, she would most zealously seek to conceal. As she is given to drink, she usually arrives half-drunk, and after two or three glasses of Madeira exposes herself in this unseemly manner. Look, she is on all fours now, like an animal. She is ridiculed and men gloat over such prostitution of incomparable beauty.'

In one startlingly noticeable respect, English sexual life during this period did not increase in desirability, even though it might do so in subtlety and organization.

Having seen what occurred during the Roman period, it need not surprise us that the violence of the first part of the century rapidly became linked to sexuality—if, indeed, it was not originally founded in it. In a period of freedom, such as the Renaissance, the Restoration—and the eighteenth century, one expects to find that the male attitude towards women is as equal, if not slightly superior beings, and that this attitude is reflected in every aspect of life. In the case of the first two periods these expectations are fulfilled. In the case of the third they are violently disappointed. The gallant of this allegedly golden age might fancy himself to be free of all controls, and so, in one sense, he was; but to his unconscious he was a perfect slave. His attitude towards women, although a profoundly and frankly sexual one; was based in hatred and hostility. The link between violence and sexuality in this period was, as I have said, strong. In this century first appear, in their really violent and most extreme forms, the three manias: 'defloration mania', the mania for girls below the age of puberty, and 'flagellomania'.

To deflower a girl can be an assault, an act of hostility. In the pornographic literature of this period, emphasis is placed on the victim's screams of pain and cries for help: the blood, the humiliation, the fear. Copulation with a girl in whom the sexual instincts are not fully aroused is, as far as she is concerned, a frightening and cruel attack. Thus, the sexual act, instead of being a source of pleasure for the participants, has become equated with the degradation of the woman, a means for the man to display his superiority and display his contempt. (Taine describes the English Don Juan as possessed of 'unyielding pride, the desire to subjugate others, the provocative love of battle, the need for ascendency, these are his dominant features.')

The demand was met by the pimps and procuresses (who were not ignorant of the numerous means by which virginity could be falsified) with a corresponding supply of 'virgins' and 'juveniles'—sometimes without the inverted commas.

From this situation, it is a short step to flagellation. The quantity of pornographic literature dealing with this perversion published during the eighteenth century almost surpasses belief.

The sadistic-masochistic instinct is present in everybody in a greater or lesser degree, and plays some part in their actual sexual relations.

Bartolinus says: 'Persians and Russians chastise their wives with blows from a stick on the posterior before they perform their marital duty. The bride in Russia would rather be without any other piece of household goods than rods. These rods are never used for punishment, but only for the purpose mentioned.'

Here the motive is quite consciously sexual, and the flagellation used merely as a prefatory to copulation—not as a sexual act in itself. In the eighteenth century this is what it shortly became, the attitude of the sadist or masochist towards the true motives for his behaviour becoming less and less honest, and more and more bound up in make-believe.

The vice spread with extreme rapidity; flagellants male and female, active and passive, heterosexual and homosexual, caught the infection. In the main, men tend towards passive flagellation, women towards active. This is not as paradoxical as it at first seems. We need to demonstrate our ascendency or subjugation only when the matter is in doubt. For the same reason, the proportion of flagellant homosexuals of both sexes is slightly higher than that among heterosexuals.

The practice of flagellation being, although astoundingly common, by no means universal, it could not be satisfied so easily as more normal desires. Thus the flagellants tended to congregate in clubs and brothels. A number of the latter, devoted entirely to activities of this kind, were soon organized by the several financially shrewd and perhaps sadistically inclined members of the corps of procuresses. The queen of these was Mrs. Theresa Berkeley, who, at her house at 28 Charlotte Street, Portland Place, 'was past mistress of her art, an expert in knowing the various whims of her male clients, which she satisfied in the most refined manner: at the same time she was an excellent business woman, and put by a considerable fortune.' (She made £10,000 in eight years, living in considerable comfort meanwhile.) 'Her arsenal of implements was immensely more complete than that of any other governess . . . in her establishment anyone provided with reasonable means could have himself beaten with canes, scourges, whips and straps; pricked with needles, half-strangled, scrubbed with many kinds of harsh brushes, scourged with nettles, currycombed, bled and tortured until he had had enough of it.' So Bloch.

On top of all this, Mrs. Berkeley invented the 'Berkeley Horse' or 'chevalet'—'It was really an adjustable ladder, which could be extended to a considerable length, and on which the victim was securely strapped, openings being left for the head and genitals. In Mrs. Berkeley's *Memoirs* there appears a copper plate, showing the Horse in use. Bloch adds details of this plate, which portrays Mrs. Berkeley with the aid of a female assistant, seated beneath the horse, attending to the requirements of a rude customer.

Clubs provided another, more satisfactory outlet for the flagellant. Here he or she could mingle with those who genuinely shared his own tastes, and were not merely simulating sadism for financial motives.

The *Bon Ton Magazine*, December 1792, describes a female flagellants' club.

'These female members are mainly married women, who, tired of marriage in its usual form, and the cold indifference which is wont to accompany it; determined by a novel method to reawaken the ecstasy which they knew at the beginning of their married life. . . . The honourable society or club to which we refer never has fewer than twelve members. At each meeting six are chastised by the other six. They draw lots for the order of procedure: then, either a written speech is read, or an extempore one delivered, on the effects of flagellation as it has been practised from the earliest age up to the present day: . . . after which the six patients take their places, and the six flagellants begin the practical demonstration. The president of the club hands to each a stout rod, and begins the chastisement herself, with any variations she likes, while the others watch. Sometimes, by order of the president, the whipping starts on the calves and goes up to the posterior, until the whole region, as Shakespeare says, from milk-white "becomes one red".' (Colour changes are undoubtedly, as Bloch has suggested, an important factor in the sexual satisfaction of flagellants.)

The schoolmastering profession has always attracted homosexual flagellants and brought out the hidden sadistic desires of those in whom they had hitherto lain dormant.

In the case of both, the true motives for their disciplinary ideas may be concealed from themselves: or from others whilst professionally engaged, but this concealment may well be dropped in private life.

Bloch has repeated the story of a curious dinner-party originally described by an anonymous author. It concerns: 'the visit of a teacher in north Yorkshire to a neighbouring colleague, a widower, who was passionately fond of the use of the cane, and who satisfied this passion in the most peculiar ways. His housekeeper was called "Mother Birch" on account of her exceptional skill in making rods with good prickles. The teller of the story found with his colleagues two other pedagogues, a Dr. S., well known as a fanatical flagellant, and a Mr. T., who looked somewhat boyish. On going into the dining-room, these met with a remarkable sight. In the four corners of the room were four candelabras, apparently held by four boys with naked posteriors. They were tied up, and the hands so fastened that it looked as if they held the candelabra. After the first course the four worthy pedagogues set themselves to flogging the bare posteriors of the boys, in which work Dr. S. and the host were the most zealous. They then sat down with great appetite, and "Dr. S. crunched the bones as if they were those of the boys whom he had punished!" The dessert was brought in by four other boys in blue jackets trimmed with silver, and white breeches. The host then took out "four beautiful little canes bound with blue ribbon" and the peculiar quartette again began their questionable activities.

Thereafter Mr. T. was bound on the "horse" and his gestures and grimaces during the punishment highly amused his three lovable colleagues. The host himself carried out the whipping of his guest, in which he employed the method of the celebrated Dr. Keate, which was very uncomfortable for the victim. Mr. T. roared with pain and begged to be let loose, which, however, did not disturb the second Dr. Keate in his favourite occupation. Dr. S. continued the flagellation of his colleague, till the poor T., half fainting with pain, was set free, on which a hand of whist finished off this edifying "little dinner".'

To escape from the world of perversion and of the brothel, the more fortunate members of society visited one of the country houses of their friends of which a number, obviously based on the *petites maisons galantes* so popular in France, were beginning to appear. Of such houses the obvious example is Medmenham.

Those men who could afford it liked to add a dash of spice and sophistication to their pleasures, and as violence, bullying and rowdyism faded from their pastimes they searched for something else to take its place. They searched, and some of them found what they required in a set of neo-religious beliefs, rites and observances which could be entwined in their orgies to give them that life without which they would soon lead to tedium, morbidity and disgust. They found Satanism.

In the seventeenth century Satanism was something too serious, too full of real dread for many members of society, for it to be treated even partially as a joke. By the beginning of the eighteenth century the terror was fading, and this is reflected in the attitude of the pamphleteers towards the clubs which they attack for practising it.

Such clubs there certainly were, which at the beginning of the century were attacked (in the first place for political reasons) and forced to disperse or to go more securely underground, but when they reappeared twenty years later the attitude towards them was different, and savoured more of mockery than of fear or loathing. The careful reversal and perversion of the ritual of the Christian Church gave the members of the Hell-Fire clubs that elaboration, that set of rules, the organization of the complicated children's game which was part of the trend I have mentioned above. The first hell-fire club, presided over by Lord Wharton, was said by the pamphleteers who launched into the attack on this and other allied clubs, to hold indecent and blasphemous orgies at Somerset House, a house in Westminster and at another in Conduit Street. The club consisted of forty members, fifteen of whom were women.

In Ireland, a Mr. Conolly held Satanistic orgies at his hunting lodge, perched on the very summit of Mt. Pelier, near Rathfarnham. The details of their orgies consist in major part of wild and improbable rumour; it was said that their ceremonies were presided over by an immense black cat, and that they called each other by names such as Old Dragon and Lady Gomorrah. (Ladies were invariably present at the meetings of this club. Their presence was in fact a condition of meeting.) They drank a mixture of whisky and butter served hot and held mock crucifixions. Finally they were broken up at some time in the 1740s by the exorcizing of their cat. A clergyman whom they had invited to attend one of their parties, and who had been offended by the animal's being served before him, prayed to such spectacular effect that the cat flew through the ceiling at fantastic speed and was never seen again. This seems to have initiated the collapse of the building, for ten years later it was nothing but a heap of ruins, and the members did not meet again.

The club was created by the Earl of Rosse, an eccentric and indefatigable rake, who brought more panache and originality to the commission of his vices than any other man of his age. Dr. Madden of Dublin, calling on Lord Rosse one day was somewhat startled when his host sprang stark naked into the room, arms and legs waving monkey-like, and after courteously expressing his pleasure at seeing the Doctor, ran to the door, where he stood exhibiting himself to the people passing by.

After initiation, the novitiate was allowed to have the fulfilment of his most sensual desires.

' 'Tis here where brightest nymphs do constantly abound to satiate our constant craving appetites; nor do we meet but when our lusts run high and nature rallying gives new force to love,' wrote the author of a broadside against this club, and from what is known of the characters of the individual members, it seems likely that he spoke the truth.

For the interval, Satanism lay quiescent. The pamphleteers turned their attention to such institutions as the Mollies' Club, a homosexual organization, who met dressed as girls at a public house in the city, and after amusing themselves with elaborate fantasy, and having refreshed themselves with copious draughts of wine, 'began to enter upon their beastly obscenities, and to take those infamous liberties with one another, that no man who is not sunk into a state of devilism can think on without blushing.' So Ward, who has dealt with this particular club at considerable length and with undisguised gusto.

Satanism, as practised by the rakes, was sleeping only, not dead. In the middle of the century there appeared the last, the most famous, and the most elaborate hell-fire club of them all.

The world of Sir Francis Dashwood and of his associates cannot be taken as typical of the times in which they lived. Indeed, by the very nature of their society they were seeking

F

an escape from reality more profound, more cloistered (but, at the same time, less symptomatic of inner disease), than that effected by any other body of rakes. They lived in an elaborate and carefully maintained dream, and for the explanation of their bizarre and almost childish games, we may seek in the character of Sir Francis himself.

In his early years he had been a member of the Dilettanti Society, a body of young men who met for the purpose of eating, drinking, and discussing the arts, in a manner which seemed to many of their contemporaries pretentious and absurd. Smollet mocked them in *Count Fathom* and so did other writers, but they both survived and flourished. They brought back from Italy memories of Palladian splendour, but they also brought back that curious eighteenth-century idea of landscape gardening which consisted in piling ruins and grottoes in elaborate confusion in the midst of stark, dead trees, thick bushy woods, and waterfalls. A Palladian temple stood side by side with a Gothic arch. This craze for the picturesque, and all the agreeable lunacies that accompanied it, were evoked in the minds of men such as Sir Francis Dashwood by the word 'Gothic'. A wave of curious romantic melancholy, of idealized medievalism, had caught the minds of the members of the Dilettanti Society, and 'Gothic' turned from a word of abuse into a word of praise.

In the middle of Buckinghamshire, overlooking one of the most beautiful valleys in England, Sir Francis Dashwood lived at West Wycombe House above the village of the same name. His house was perhaps less splendid, less extravagant in its magnificence than the houses of some other gentlemen, but it made up for this in the elaboration of the gardens; and the statues and temples with which they were decorated. He had laid out one part of the garden in the shape of a woman, with much suggestive grouping of pillars and bushes, an expensive smutty joke which could not be appreciated fully until the invention of the aeroplane. John Wilkes, who visited West Wycombe, gives an account of the things he saw there, at a period shortly following the building of the church 'on the top of a hill, for the convenience of the town at the bottom of it.'

The nature of Lord Despencer's gardens gave Wilkes no better idea of his morals than the position of his church did of his piety. He noted particularly a remarkable temple 'dedicated to Tristram Shandy's Tetragammaton.' Wilkes remarks that, although his lordship's devotion to this object was probably not fervent, he was at least consistent in it, and goes on to mention a picture which used to hang in the King's Arms Tavern, Palace Yard, presented by Sir Francis to the Dilettanti Club. In this painting, he is portrayed, in the habit of a Franciscan friar, kneeling before the Venus de Medicis, 'his gloating eyes fixed as in a trance on what the modesty of nature seems most anxious to conceal, and a bumper in his hand with the words MATRI SANCTORUM in capitals. The glory too, which till then had only enriched the heads of Our Saviour and his Apostles, is made to beam upon that hallowed spot, and seems to pierce the gloom of Maidenhead Thicket.'

Wilkes then describes the temple mentioned above. The entrance was 'the same entrance by which we all came into the world and the door was what some idle wits have called the door of life.'

There were in the gardens no busts of philosophers or statesmen, but there was 'a most indecent statue of the unnatural satyr', and on the top of the temple there was a 'particular column skirted with very pretty underwood, the Cyprian Myrtle, etc.', the meaning of which, said Wilkes, he could not find out. He was not impressed by the contents of the house, but admired 'a very moral picture of a maid stealing to her master's bed, laying at the same time her fingers upon her lips, as though she were the Dea Angerona of West Wycombe.'

From Hannan's *Four views of West Wycombe House* it is possible to gain some further, although possibly embroidered and idealized notion of the house. Statues and urns are scattered in profusion about the gardens, an artificial waterfall tumbles over a recumbent Neptune, quantities of elegantly dressed people wander about the lawns consuming cups of tea, in the distance a pleasure boat floats on the lake.

Sir Francis had inherited the building from his father, and at the time of his membership of the Dilettanti, had altered and redecorated it with the aid of the architect Nicholas Revett, and the painter Joseph Borgnis. He had already gained a reputation for wildness and debauchery. He was reputed to have joined one of the early hell-fire clubs, it is thought the one of which Lord Sandwich was a member. He had gone, conventionally, on the Grand Tour, but had taken pains to make it as unconventional as possible. He ripped his way across Europe, leaving behind him a trail of rumour, amazement and notoriety. A taste for the blasphemous and profane appeared; he ridiculed the tutor who accompanied him round the shrines of Rome in the hopes of turning him into a devout Catholic. In Rome he played a joke which might well have had serious consequences for him. On Good Friday, in the Sistine Chapel, the penitents scourged themselves, gently, to the accompaniment of feigned cries of pain. Sir Francis joined the queue, received a miniature scourge, entered the chapel and concealed himself behind a pillar, until the penitents had stripped to the waist. He then drew from its place of concealment beneath his coat, a large horsewhip, with which he proceeded to lay about right and left until the church echoed with screams of agony and terrified cried of '*il diavolo!*'

At the time when he perpetrated this practical joke, Dashwood was no longer a boy. Indeed, the clue to his crazy character may lie partly in the fact that he never grew up. He may, although I doubt this, have been certifiably insane. One by one the visitors to Medmenham tired, and ceased to attend the orgies of St. Francis, but the founder himself kept it up until the bitter end.

Even when a member of the Dilettanti, Sir Francis began to show signs of the traits in his character which were to lead him step by step towards Medmenham. There was a rumour of practices savouring of the black arts in connexion with the activities of this club in its early days, and Sir Francis was certainly able to indulge in his mania for wearing fancy dress. The President wore ceremonial robes in the form of a magnificent crimson Roman toga. The Arch-Master wore a similar costume but with 'a rich Hungarian cap' and a long sword. Dashwood met a congenial spirit in the person of John Montague, Lord Sandwich, a fellow member, and the future 'Jemmy Twitcher' of the pamphleteers. His gangling figure, the weak lustful face wearing an ingratiating but insincere smile, could be seen loping gracelessly about London, as if, said contemporary wits, he was trying to go down both sides of the street at the same time. It was said of him that 'no man ever carried the art of seduction to so enormous a height.' He was 'as mischievous as a monkey and as lecherous as a goat.' He was 'mean to his mistresses and treacherous to his friends.' He was 'universally hated.' His talk was 'spattered with coarse expressions and smutty *double entendres*.' But Sir Francis liked him. Besides the fondness for drink, women and profanity which they both had in common, he, like Sir Francis, had spent some time at Constantinople, and shared Dashwood's passion for the Turks.

The Divan Club resulted from this passion, and Sir Francis and Lord Sandwich were among the earliest members. Little is known of the activities of this club except that it involved the complicated children's games and dressing-up which seem to have become a feature of every club to which Sir Francis belonged. He and Lord Sandwich were painted in Turkish robes, toasting, as in more than one portrait of him, a prostrate and minute Venus. The hand which is not holding the goblet is making a discreet but unmistakably obscene gesture. The uniform of the club was a set of green and crimson robes and an aquamarine turban, but there is no evidence that any member other than Lord Sandwich and Dashwood ever wore them. From the portraits mentioned above arose the confusion with the costume of the friars of Medmenham, which has led some writers to describe the latter as 'Turkish robes'. The

Divan soon faded and died owing to the lack of enthusiasm of its members, but it marked a definite step on the road to Medmenham. Before the collapse of the Divan Club in 1746, another future friar of Medmenham had joined the Dilettanti. This was none other than George Bubb Dodington, future Baron Melcombe. This engaging grotesque, whose vast conceit exhibited itself in the form of self-parody; the butt of the cartoonists with his huge belly, his swaying dewlap and his ridiculous button nose, was the eldest of all the Friars of Medmenham, being over sixty when he first visited the abbey. In his youth he had built an enormous house at Eastbury on the fruits of his inheritance. Laid out on a grandiose and geometric design, this splendid building housed a collection of exotic but tawdry furniture. Not a single picture decorated the walls. Here, in the evenings, Bubb would sit, reading aloud to the ladies in his unctuous, fruity voice some of the more indecent passages from Shakespeare. In later life, more debauched, more bombastic, this would-be Wicked Uncle built another house at Hammersmith on the banks of the river, and named it 'La Trappe'. Here he would entertain as his guests, whom he dressed in the habits of monks, many of the famous of his day. The drawing-room boasted a marble chimney-piece hung with imitation icicles, and in the gardens there was a temple to Venus.

Sir Francis continued on his colourful way. It was said that 'he far exceeded in licentiousness anything exhibited since the days of Charles II.' Horace Walpole remarked that he seldom found him sober. He was reputed to have slept with every whore of note in the town. He also played at political intrigue, and it was in this sphere of his life that he met Paul Whitehead, possibly the principal mover in the foundation of Medmenham.

Younger than Sir Francis, the poet had the appearance of being many years older, with such untiring energy had he pursued the accomplishment of his unspeakable desires. This mean, conceited, repellent figure, having emerged from prison, where he had spent a large part of his early life, having backed a theatrical manager's bill for which he had proved unable to pay, took up the profession of political hack. He married a half-wit for her money, and the fortune she brought him enabled him to indulge himself more or less to his satisfaction. Sir Francis tolerated, but openly ridiculed him, and when he died, gave him a comic funeral at West Wycombe.

Whitehead had organized an elaborate and libellous parody of the annual march of the Freemasons. A convoy of tramps, beggars and shoeblacks and cripples, hired for the occasion, capered down the Strand past Somerset House, bearing indecent insignia on poles, and accompanied by an escort of rake-hells beating on kitchen utensils and blowing trumpets.

This incident delighted Dashwood, and from then onwards the bust of Whitehead stood among the Venuses and Satyrs of West Wycombe.

With such a conglomeration of personalities the foundation of Medmenham could not be long delayed. One circumstance only was wanting, and that was the meeting between Dashwood and Francis Duffield. Duffield shared Dashwood's wildness and his peculiar fancy for the arts, and between themselves they discussed the idea of a brotherhood. Duffield was one of the first members. The nature of his family house could not fail to appeal to Sir Francis, a ruined church would form the ideal background for his play-acting, and some time in 1752 or '53 the lease was signed, Sir Francis moved in, and Duffield moved out. Transported with schoolboy enthusiasm for this new toy, Dashwood drove Nicholas Revett down to Medmenham, and rushed about the house and gardens discussing possible alterations. The house was a low, rambling, reddish-coloured and sadly deserted-looking building, but there was always the background of the old abbey.

Work was soon begun, the workmen being brought secretly from London and smuggled back again by night. The servants were sworn not to speak to anybody in the district, and never to reveal the nature of the singular decorations being installed. Nevertheless the rumours escaped.

A ruined tower, a Gothic arch, cloisters, ivy-covered pillars were erected to give colour to Dashwood's dream. He discovered in the remains of the old abbey church a figure of the Virgin and Child which he removed to a niche in his new ruined tower. Over the eastern entrance to the house he painted the famous motto, '*Fay Ce Que Vouldra*', from Rabelais' abbey of Thelema.

The family chapel of the Duffields was converted into a private shrine for St. Francis. After the 'alterations', no one but Sir Francis and Duffield, and the painter and architect, Borgnis and Revett, were permitted to enter it. The ceiling was covered with indecent frescoes, the walls with brutal caricatures of the twelve apostles. At the end of the room, behind the altar rails, stood the parody of a Holy Altar.

Wilkes and Walpole have described the house and gardens in their finished condition. There appeared also some articles in the issues of the *Town and Country Magazine* for 1769 and 1773. Wilkes is probably the most reliable, as he was for some time, until his estrangement from the other friars, a member of the brotherhood.

'Over the grand staircase was the famous inscription, "*Fay Ce Que Vouldra*", from Rabelais' Abbey of Theleme. At the end of the passage was "*Aude Hospes, Contemnere Opes*". At one end of the refectory was Harpocrates, the Egyptian god of silence, at the other, the goddess Angerona, that the same duty might be enjoined to both sexes.

The garden, the grove, the orchard, the neighbouring woods, all spoke the loves and frailties of the younger monks, who seem at least to have sinned naturally. You saw in one place:

"*Ici pama de joie des mortels le plus heureux.*"

In another, very imperfectly:

"*Mourut un amant sur le sein de la dame.*"

152

In a third:

"En cet endroit mille baisers furent donnes ei milles autres rendus."

Against a fine old oak was:

"Hic satyrum naias victorem victa subegit."

At the entrance to a cave was Venus stooping to pull a thorn from her foot. The statue turned from you, and over the two nether hills of snow were these lines from Virgil:

"Hic locus est ubi se via fundit in ambas
Hac iter Elysium nobis: at laeva malorum,
Exercet poenas et ad impia Tartars mittit. . . ."

On the inside of the cave, over a mossy couch was the following exhortation:

"Ite, agite O juvenes panter sudate medullis
Omnibus inter vos; non murmure vestra columbae
Branchae non hederae, non vincant oscula conchae."

The favourite doctrine of the abbey is certainly not penitence for in the centre of the orchard was a grotesque figure, and in his hand a reed stood flaming, to use Milton's expression, and you might trace out:

"PENI TENTO

non

PENITENTI"

On the pedestal was a whimsical representation of Trophonius' cave, from whence all creatures were said to come out melancholy. Among that strange, dismal group you might however remark a cock crowing and a Carmelite laughing. The words "*gallum gallinaceum et sacerdotem gratis*" were alone legible.

Near the abbey was a small neat temple erected to Cloacine with the inscription "This chapel of ease was founded in the year 1760".'

There is no reason, apart from possible political animosity, to doubt Wilkes's description of the gardens of Medmenham. There were certainly others at this epoch which contained similar graffiti. Stowe House, for example, was reputed to possess a chapel, the walls of which were covered with indecent Latin poems of a kind 'inconceivable even to the most lewd imagination.' Sir Francis obtained most of his sculptural indecencies from the Charron brothers of Leghorn.

Walpole and the *Town and Country Magazine* are more informative about the inside of the house. The common-room was stocked with cards, chessboards, backgammon boards and other entertainments, and decorated with portraits of the Kings of England. Over the face of Henry VIII a piece of paper had been pasted to signify their dislike for him. There were also several paintings of the monks and nuns, and round the room hung the habits of each brother on a peg with the pseudonym of the owner. The habits, said Walpole, rather contemptuously, were more like a waterman's than a monk's, and consisted of a white hat, a white jacket and white trousers. The prior had a red hat like a cardinal's and a red bonnet trimmed with rabbit skin. The library contained a large selection of pornographic books, bound in covers bearing such titles as *Sherlock on Death* and *The Book of Common Prayer*. . . . 'Nor could the celebrated collection of the debauched and dissolute Popes, Alexander and Julius, be by any means compared with it.'

In the room above the chapel, the drawing-room, there were 'two or three long drinking-sofas covered with silk damask, constructed upon the plan of the Romans when at the height of their luxuriance and effeminacy.' This room was specially decorated at the 'Grand Gala' in a manner 'intended to convey and inspire sentiments of immorality and lewdness.'

Much of the remainder of the decorations of the house must be left to the imagination. Johnstone, the author of *Chrysal, or the Adventures of a Guinea*, gives some further hints. This is a satirical novel, but there is no doubt that Johnstone spoke with somebody who attended the Medmenham orgies.

'There was not a vice for the practising which he did not make provision. The cellars were stored with the choicest wines, the larders with the delicacies of every climate.' The cells, although otherwise fairly plain, were 'fitted up for all purposes of lasciviousness, for which proper objects were also provided.'

The abbey was ready, and awaited only the arrival of the friars. . . .

The friars came readily enough. Languidly debauched they rolled along the road to Medmenham in their gilded coaches. Lord Sandwich, Bubb Dodington, Duffield, Whitehead, the Vansittarts, Thomas Potter.

Handsome, witty, utterly depraved, Potter, the son of the Archbishop of Canterbury, was regarded even in the eighteenth century, as wicked, vicious, and spendthrift beyond belief. His health completely undermined at the age of thirty-five by the existence that he led, he suffered from constant fits of depression and hypochondria. A friend of John Wilkes, it was he who urged the satirist to Medmenham. Potter must have been one of the only men with influence over Wilkes, just as Dashwood was one of the only men with influence over Potter. At any rate, whether at the command of St. Francis or from desire for still untasted pleasures, he joined the foremost of the pilgrims bound for Medmenham.

Before condemning or despising the friars, it should be remembered that they probably did not meet much above twice a year (there is considerable divergence of opinion on this point), and then only for a fortnight at a time, otherwise their society could never have lasted as long as it did. Even so, it is amazing that they kept it up for so long, and without a powerful driving motive they would never have done so. It is hard to conceive that the motive of the brethren of St. Francis can have been anything other than their excessively strong sexuality, than that they were physically and mentally obsessed by their sexual fantasies. Their Satanistic games, with the elaborate schoolboy ritual, should be taken as a spice, or as a cloak of romanticism, which made their indulgences in the pleasures of the flesh more palatable to swallow. Even in that age of libidinousness, they could not take their sex neat the whole time, and this, perhaps, is what places the Medmenham brethren above their contemporaries and what saves them from our contempt.

It will not do to dismiss too lightly the devil-worshipping side of the Medmenham orgies. In Satanism they found one kind of escapism, just as in their nuns they found another. Nevertheless an examination of the characters of the brotherhood cannot fail to leave one with the impression that in the presence of the sisterhood they found the most endearing aspect of life at the abbey.

At the beginning of the present century the minute-book kept by Paul Whitehead, and recording the *divertissements* of the society, was burnt by an officious Edwardian, who took it upon himself to decide that the book was too obscene to be allowed to continue to exist. Our information as to what, exactly, occurred has to be pieced together from a variety of sources. That something did occur, only one man has attempted to deny. Dr. Benjamin Bates, who in his youth was one of the friars, in old age indignantly denied that anything scandalous took place. He was never one of the more faithful brethren, and possibly for his own comfort he preferred to erase unsavoury and inconvenient details from his mind. The weight of the evidence is against him.

The letters of the brethren are disappointingly discreet, and in communicating with one another, they remain on surprisingly formal terms. Nevertheless the rumours leaked out.

There were two orders of friars, the superior, and the inferior. The inferior consisted chiefly of distinguished local visitors for whom there were cells enough on the special occasions when they were invited. It was rumoured that the superior order slept not in beds, but in gigantic cradles. This story is thought to have originated with a Miss Berry, who, on a visit to the abbey, noticed an old cradle belonging to the caretaker, and concocted from the incident this pleasing and sinister fantasy.

Apart from the caretaker, there were no regular servants. Those required for the serving and preparation of the meals were hired by the day, dismissed, and replaced on the following day by fresh.

The food was probably rich, plentiful and exotic. The anonymous author of *Hell upon Earth; or the Town in an Uproar*, attacks the eating habits of such societies as Sir Francis's, and gives as a typical menu:

Soupe de Sante
Soupe au Bourgeoise

Carp au Court Bouillon

Pupton of Partridge
Cullets à la Maine

Beef à la Tremblade
Fricasse of Salamanders
Huffle of Chickens

A Stewed Lyon

Pain Perdu
Oysters à la Danube
Blanc Manger

The 'nuns' were recruited from the London stews, and

conveyed in closed wagons to Medmenham. Sir Francis's association with Mrs. 'Hell-Fire' Stanhope here came in handy, but later when the cat was out of the bag, and local rumour was rife, they succeeded in obtaining an adequate number from local wantons, who, having heard of the luxury and wealth of the monks as well as of their carnality, were not unnaturally ready to meet them half-way.

The nuns wore small silver brooches engraved with the words 'Love and Friendship'. Not all of them were whores or local girls. Friars sometimes introduced ladies to the society.

These ladies were allowed to appear masked, at first, in order that they might scrutinize the company and avoid any unfortunate meeting with husband or betrothed. A physician, a surgeon and a midwife were in attendance, and should one of the sisterhood become pregnant as a result of her devotions, she was permitted to lie in at the abbey 'where they may retire in seasonable time.'

The nuns only attended on nights when the superior orders were alone present, but on such nights their presence was made a condition of meeting. The office of Abbot was taken in rotation, the Abbot of the day having certain privileges, such as first choice of women, and various corresponding duties such as the inspection of the cellars to make sure that there was a more than adequate supply of wine, and of the cells to make sure that they were equipped with everything that the brethren might find necessary. The post of Abbot might be temporary, but that of Grand Master was permanent. It was he who officiated at the sinister preparatory ceremonies in the chapel, who administered a perverted sacrament to the Medmenham baboon, who initiated new brothers into the order, who offered libations to the Devil.

These self-imposed duties performed, they settled down with a clearer conscience to the enjoyment of their pleasures. Toast followed toast throughout the long meal in the refectory until, replete with wine and 'stewed lyon', brother after brother seized a nun and at the table or in the cells, or on the lawn lit by the setting summer sun, worshipped not the Devil nor yet a baboon, but the goddess to whom the garden temple was erected.

The abbey continued to function for a surprising length of time, and although the majority of the brothers, as the years passed, tired and came no more, yet when dissolution ultimately overtook Medmenham, it was due to political causes, not the ennui of the participants. In the mud-slinging which followed the arrest of Wilkes in connexion with the publication of No. 45 of the *North Briton*, a gobbet flew in the direction of Medmenham. With dissension among the friars, with Lord Sandwich reading aloud to the House of Lords 'The Essay on Woman' in tones of feigned prudery (thus providing a line for the *Beggars' Opera*, 'That Jemmy should peach me, I own surprised me!'), the gradually declining members decided that limelight was too strong for their aged eyes, and went (literally) underground.

When Sir Francis had had a road constructed from motives of pretended (or possibly genuine) philanthropy, the chalk for the construction had been taken from the hill at West Wycombe, and this provided him and his colleagues with a ready-made network of caves. The caves had a Gothic façade with pointed and pillared arches carved in the chalk, and in their damp and labyrinthine depths the last orgies of the Medmenham brotherhood were held.

But Sir Francis had a newer project afoot, the church mentioned by Wilkes in the passage (already quoted) in which he describes the gardens at West Wycombe. This fantastic building, designed probably as a central point from which to view the estate, topped with its gigantic gilded ball, poised like some bizarre lighthouse above its village, aroused amazement but not gratitude in the hearts of the parishioners. More like a ballroom than a church, as one visitor remarked, it had no seats for the villagers, but this deficiency was made up for by the presence of wine-coolers in the aisles for Lord Despencer and his family.

When Bubb Dodington, old, miserable, and surrounded by quack doctors, blundering along a passage at Eastbury, tripped and, falling on his nose, rolled noisily down the kitchen stairs, he had time to insert in his will before he died, a clause bequeathing to Sir Francis the sum of £500 for the purpose of erecting a temple to house his, Bubb's, ashes. The building which Dashwood was thus enabled to append to his church became the mausoleum of most of the friars of Medmenham.

But the days of Medmenham were over. Sir Francis became, of physical necessity, more sober. He sat in the gold ball on top of his church, drinking milk punch, plotting incompetently, and gazing at his magnificent view, until on 11 December, 1781, he died.

His fantasies lingered behind him. Many of them, of inferior manufacture despite their ingenuity, crumbled, like the temple mentioned by Wilkes, to dust; but in the village it is rumoured that up at West Wycombe House, there is a room which has been locked since Queen Victoria's day, so indecent are its contents.

Before leaving the eighteenth century, I would like to mention two clubs, a parent and a daughter institution, that existed in Scotland during the last three-quarters of the century. I mean the Most Ancient and Puissant Order of the Beggar's Benison and Merryland, and the Wig Club.

At Anstruther, in Fifeshire, the Earls of Anstruther lived at Castle Dreel. In the fourteenth century they were already established there, and they and a group of local gentry took it upon themselves to form a society for the protection of fishing rights against English, Flemish and French interlopers. They used as their centre the Isle of May. In the twelfth century there had been a monastery on this island. The monks left after a comparatively short space of time, but for a period there was a chaplain on the island to take care of the relics, amongst which was the coffin of St. Adrian. It was said that to touch this coffin was a sure cure for barrenness. Pilgrims who went to the island received the blessing, 'Be fruitful, and multiply'. There were rumours that chastity was not among the virtues of the chaplains.

This piece of history is of considerable relevance in view of the remarkable recrudescence of phallic worship of a kind normally only associated with pagan and primitive fertility festivals, which occurred in this part of Scotland during the eighteenth and nineteenth centuries. It is still more remarkable, when one considers that it was still flourishing long after the pendulum had started on its return swing towards 'Victorianism'.

The origin of the name 'Beggar's Benison' derives from a probably legendary anecdote of James V. It is said of this king that he liked to travel about the country incognito, disguised as a bagpiper or beggar.

One day, when he was journeying to Anstruther Fair, he came to Dreel Burn, over which there was no bridge. By the stream there happened to be standing a beggar-maid. This girl amiably hoisted the king on to her back and carried him across. When James paid the girl a gold sovereign, she gave him her benison:

> 'May your purse naer be toom
> And your horn aye in bloom.'

When James had arrived at Castle Dreel, and made himself known to the inhabitants, so delighted was he with this experience, which he described to them, that he formed them then and there into a humorous order of knighthood called 'The Beggar's Benison'.

The modern order, with which we are here concerned, was founded in 1732. This date appears on two of the seals. The meetings took place twice a year, at Candlemas and on St. Andrew's Day, two to four novices being admitted each year. They began the session with a light dinner, after which they adjourned to the 'temple'.

The records of the initiation ceremonies still exist, but if there was not corroborative evidence in the objects in the Kavanagh Collection (now in the possession of Mrs. Canch Kavanagh) one would hesitate to accept the description as the literal truth.

The 'sovereign' presided. He wore a green satin sash on which were written the words, 'Sovereign Beggar's Benison'. All the other members also wore a sash and a medal. On one side of these medals is Adonis, Venus and Cupid, on the other Adonis and Venus. Some of the later medals bear the blessing of the monks of May, 'Be fruitful and multiply'.

The ceremony of initiation began when the Remembrancer brought out the Test Platter and placed on a high stool in the centre of the room.

The platter in the Kavanagh Collection is oval, about eight inches long, and on it are the words 'Beggar's Benison 1732. The Way of a Man with a Maid. Test Platter.'

The novice was then brought in, having been prepared for the ceremony. As he entered a small silver horn was blown, a pun on the beggar lass's benison. It is marked with the words 'My breath is strange. Lev. x5. 16. 17.' The reference is to the passage in Leviticus dealing with the laws of purification, and has a bearing on the ceremony, the nature of which, as had probably been guessed, was autoerotic and exhibitionistic. A statement scratched on the base of the platter substantiates this theory.

At the conclusion of the ceremony a toast was drunk from two phallic wine-glasses, seven inches in height (now in the Kavanagh Collection).

After the toast the novice was told to select a passage from the Song of Solomon, and to read it aloud, with comments. For this purpose a special Bible was provided by the order, the numerous indecent passages in this book were all marked, and examples of erotic prose and verse are written on the flyleaf. The Bible was locked with two different keys, one belonging to the parent society, the other to the branch.

These keyholes were made of gold, and carved in the form

of two vulvas, crossed with the words '*Lignum Scientiae Boni et Mali*'.

Once initiated, the new member was arrayed in the regalia of the society and drank the toast to 'the beggar maid and joy'.

A banquet then followed, and this appears to have been held in Saturnalian mood. Lewd songs were sung, indecent toasts drunk, erotic curios passed from hand to hand.

Some time in the course of the evening the new member received his diploma. This was in the form of a punning travesty of a ship's licence, and bestowed upon him 'full powers and privileges of Ingress, Egress and Regress from and to, and to and from all the Harbours, Creeks, Havens and inlets upon the coast of our . . . territories at his pleasure.'

Some time during the course of the evening the arcana and a girl of the vicinity were 'shown off'.

The seal of the most Puissant Order was appended. This is of obviously skilled workmanship and design. The seal has a phallus and purse against the background of an anchor. The seal of the Edinburgh branch is basically of the same design. There are two seals of earlier date, much simpler in design and execution, with the words:

ANSTRUTHER

BEGGAR'S

love's

cave.

BENISON

1732

and two others, the most superior in workmanship with a heart and vulva, and the words 'Sight improves delight. Beggar's Benison, Anstruther', the other portraying a phallic lighthouse with a vulviform base, flanked by two pelicans.

The order was not dissolved until St. Andrew's Day, 1836, less than a year before Victoria came to the throne. Not the least remarkable thing about the society was that its members, as well as being composed of both political parties, were almost all members of the local gentry, living within a short radius of Castle Dreel.

The relationship between the Beggar's Benison and the Wig Club was a curious one, for though the Edinburgh branch was founded by discontented members of the Beggar's Benison, who carried off with them the most valued treasure of the parent society, many members of one club were members of the other, and friendly relationships seem to have been maintained.

In 1775 Lords Moray and Aboyne left the society, taking with them the club wig. The truth about the composition of this object will probably never be known, but at the time of its transfer to Edinburgh an aura of erotic legend had gathered about it. It was claimed by the order that the wig had been given to the Moray family by Charles II in gratitude for services rendered, and that it was entirely composed of the pubic hair of Charles's mistresses. How likely a tale this may be, I leave to the reader to judge; but made of somebody's pubic hair it certainly was, and each new member was required to obtain a contribution from his mistress to incorporate into the wig.

At the ceremonies of the Wig Club, which were similar in nature to those of the Beggar's Benison, each member was allowed to kiss the wig, and wear it for a short space of time.

The members of the Beggar's Benison, undismayed, later began collecting material for a wig made from the hair of the mistresses of George IV. Hanoverian energy could not keep pace with Stuart, and all that exists of this wig is a few wisps in a snuff-box with the label 'Hair from the Mons Veneris of a Royal Courtesan of George IV. . . .'

Also in the Kavanagh collection, and so far unmentioned, is a hollow metal phallus, seven inches long, and painted. What the exact purpose of this object may have been is not known. It has been suggested that it may have been constructed in the latter years of the club so that members could cover their own organs from motives of modesty. This seems unlikely.

But changing the times certainly were. The rakes' clubs were becoming respectable. A new spirit was coming over society, and whilst vice might continue to flourish it would have to do so in deeper, murkier, and better hidden channels.

This change had begun a great deal earlier than most people suppose. As early as 1757 the 'Society for the Reformation of Manners' had been started by the enterprising few (although it was bankrupted five years later after being convicted of hiring false testimony).

George III issued a 'Proclamation against Vice' and the opinions expressed in this were given material support by the 'Proclamation Society' (founded 1789). From then on the societies came thick and fast, and although the Orthodox Church might not match the medieval in its prohibitive and propagandist activities, the Wesleyan Church almost surpassed it. This reaction against liberty ended in the attitude towards life usually described as 'Victorian'.

The Romantic Movement, which on the continent was expressed in a variety of forms, in England was confined to the literary and the artistic. Sexual expression of their beliefs was impossible for the Romantics, so outnumbered and out-organized were they by the Wesleyans and their associates. (I am, of course, picturing a psychological rather than a physical battle.)

The Victorians knew that sex existed, and that it would continue to exist; but they determined that it should exist out of sight. Like the water-closet, it was necessary to life whether one liked it or not; but, like the water-closet, it did not belong in the drawing-room.

The disadvantages of this belief are obvious. If sex is filth —and this was the category to which the Victorians assigned it—then filth it was, and if it took the form, in fact and in pornographic literature, of perverse and hideous fantasy, they had only themselves to blame. In the circumstances it could not be wondered if all the undesirable features of eighteenth-century sexual life—the flagellation brothels, the traffic in virgins and juveniles—remained as a monument to their misguidedness.

SIX

THE EIGHTEENTH CENTURY
ON THE CONTINENT

I T is all very well for Taine to make the crushing and sweeping
criticism of the English rake contained in the previous chapter.
His accusations were largely justified, certainly. What is to be
doubted is whether the description should be confined to
English gallants alone.

Misconceptions about the eighteenth century on this subject
are twofold. It is held by some, without much justification,
that vicious acts at this period were performed with elegance
and taste. This may have been true in the case of a few men;
of what period is it not? It was not true, in England of the
majority. This we have seen from the previous chapter. But
for every xenophobe there is a xenophile, and there are plenty
who like to think that what is wrong in England has been
taken care of by the more sagacious Continentals. Casanova,
they tenaciously fancy, was a very different person to Lord
Sandwich. How unrelated to the facts this notion is, it is the
purpose of the following chapter to show.

In the course of an objective and analytical consideration
of the characters of two symbolic persons, I hope incidentally
to throw some light on the problem whether the orgy (the orgy
of the rebel) can *ever* be regarded as a 'normal' form of sexual
behaviour. I beg readers to bear this consideration in mind
before accusing me of picking my facts to suit my case, and to
remember that the conventional symbolism of the two is, by
most people's standards, exceedingly diverse.

Giacomo Girolamo Casanova di Seingalt died in 1798 at
the age of seventy-three, leaving behind him his enormous

169

memoirs, written apparently for his own pleasure, and without thought of publication.

The son of actor parents, he passed what would now be described as an unhappy childhood. He was originally intended for the Church, but soon revealed his unfitness for this profession. (In later life he became a Freemason, and throughout the memoirs, even incorporated into his seductions, there are recurring instances of the cabalistic balderdash in which, apparently, Casanova more or less wholeheartedly believed.) He had in the end no regular profession, being at one time the director of a government lottery, and at another (1774–1782) a police spy in Venice. Throughout his life he displayed a passion for gambling.

The memoirs deal almost exclusively with Casanova's amorous conquests, together with rather Pepysian revelations of his own state of mind. But Casanova was a more tortuous character than Pepys. Examining the memoirs one instantly receives the impression that one is reading pornographic *fiction*.

Every incident stinks of fantasy, but Casanova's veracity, where checkable, is unblemished, and he must be treated as a truthful man, and his memoirs as fact.

The first thing that struck me when I analysed the various situations and episodes contained in the memoirs is the perpetual recurrence of one situation, a recurrence, in fact, of almost suspicious exactness.

Casanova had, it is quite clear from his own account, either in theory or in fact, a marked drive towards performing the sexual act with one woman in the presence of another. For example, in the case of Helen and Hedwig, two girls whom he deflowers in the presence of each other:

'I overwhelmed them with happiness for several hours, passing five or six times from one to the other before I was exhausted. In the intervals, seeing them to be docile and desirous, I made them execute Aretin's most complicated postures, which amused them beyond words. We kissed whatever took our fancy' (particulars follow in the original, not reproducible here). She was delighted, and watched the process to the end with all the curiosity of a doctor.'

Here Casanova seems to have projected his own attitude on to Hedwig. *He* is the one with the clinical and rather morbid interest in the details of copulation.

The same situation, or one closely similar to it, occurs in the case of Annette and Veronique.

'Veronique resigned herself to the passive part which her younger sister imposed on her, and turning aside, she leant her head on her hand, disclosing a breast which would have excited the coldest of men, and bade me begin my attack on Annette. It was no hard task she laid upon me, for I was all on fire, and was certain of pleasing her as long as she looked at me. As Annette was short-sighted, she could not distinguish in the heat of the action which way I was looking, and I succeeded in getting my right hand free, without her noticing me, and I was thus able to communicate a pleasure as real, though not as acute as that enjoyed by her sister. Whenever the coverlet was disarranged, Veronique took the trouble to replace it, and this offered me, as if by accident, a new spectacle. She saw how I enjoyed the sight of her charms, and her eye brightened. At last, full of unsatisfied desire, she showed me all the treasures which nature had given her, just as I had finished with Annette for the fourth time. She might well think that I was only rehearsing for the following night, and her fancy must have painted her coming joys in the brightest colours.'

And yet again at Casanova's 'Oyster Suppers'. These were parties, given by Casanova to two nuns, Armelline and Emilie, to whom he fed enormous quantities of oysters and champagne. He makes the room so hot that the girls have to remove their outer clothes. Then, whilst playing a game in which one person removes an oyster from another's mouth by suction, he contrives to drop an oyster, accidentally on purpose, down the front of first one girl's corset, then the other's. This results in interesting explorations of recovery and is followed by a comparison, first visual then sensory, of the comparative dimensions of the two pairs of legs. It is interesting from another point of view that this adventure with the nuns took place during the time of the carnival.

An exaggerated form of the same thing can be seen in the incident of the supper at Bassi's (a temporary business associate of Casanova's).

'When the supper and wine had sufficiently raised my spirits I devoted my attention to Bassi's daughter, who let me do what I liked, while her father and mother only laughed, and the silly Harlequin fretted and fumed at not being able to take the same liberties with his Dulcinea. But, at the end of the supper, when I had made the girl in a state of nature, I myself being dressed like Adam before he ate the fatal apple, Harlequin rose and, taking his sweetheart's arm, was going to draw her away. I imperiously told him to sit down, and he obeyed me in amazement, contenting himself with turning his back. His sweetheart did not follow his example, and so placed herself on the pretext of defending my victim, that she increased my enjoyment, while my vagrant hand did not seem to displease her.

'The scene excited Bassi's wife, and she begged her husband to give her a proof of his love for her, to which request he acceded, whilst modest Harlequin sat by the fire with his head in his hands.

'The Alsatian was in a highly excited state, and took advantage of her lover's position to grant me all I wished, so I proceeded to execute the great work on her, and the violent movements of her body proved that she was taking as active a part in it as myself.'

The general pattern should by now be becoming clear. Casanova is just as much, if not even more, interested in the reactions of the spectators or spectator, than in those of the person with whom he is actually performing the sexual act. He was, it can be fairly stated, an exhibitionist. It is true that exhibitionism, particularly in the legal sense, is sometimes performed with the intention of shocking or of causing pain and embarrassment. This is not always the case. On the contrary, in the words of Dr. Lindesay Neustatter (*Encyclopaedia of Medical Practice*): 'It may be his intention to produce a profound and pleasing effect.' In this context another remark by the same physician may suitably be quoted. 'The history often shows that by the age of five years, many exhibitionists have strong sexual feelings. They possibly also show the beginnings of other perversions, such as sadism.'

Sadism if reduced to its basic principle is little more than the desire to impress in the most obvious and extreme way, the mark of one's own personality on the external world.

The money element in Casanova's life is very prominent, and accompanying this an extreme awareness of class differences. He may like the idea of conquering women by his personal charm and physical attraction. He prefers the idea of buying them.

Half the point of the Bassi incident in Casanova's eyes is that Harlequin is humiliated and pained. At the end of the orgy he makes special mention of the pleasure and sense of power which he derived from paying off the human beings with whom he had been toying.

When frustrated in love he becomes petulant and violent. La Charpillon, who admittedly teased him intolerably, is knocked down, beaten, half-strangled, scratched, and kicked on the nose when she proves unmoved and unflattered by Casanova's attentions. He also displays a minor streak of voyeurism, with which perversion exhibitionism is frequently associated. Casanova, so far from being the healthy extroverted model of virile sexuality, begins to assume many of the characteristics of a neurotic pervert. The incident of 'Goudar's chair' (which savours more strongly than any other incident in the whole work of fantasy rather than of fact) completes this impression.

The chair was, according to Casanova, in appearance a

very ugly but otherwise ordinary armchair. However, if a woman (or a man) were to sit down in it, 'two springs catch the two arms and hold them tightly, two others separate the legs and the fifth (spring) lifts up the seat.'

After this description, Gouda (Angelo not Sara) sits down in the seat, and 'the springs came into position and forced him into the position of a woman in labour.' Casanova, after toying mentally with the possible uses to which he could put this piece of apparatus—e.g. the humiliation and capture of La Charpillon, rejects the idea of purchasing it—too unflattering to his self-esteem—all the same the idea clearly took a hold on his imagination.

Perhaps if one adds the incident in which Casanova copulates with a hunchbacked woman (with difficulties, which he details with his usual medico-anatomical absorption) the picture is sufficiently clearly that of a man neither pleasant nor normal.

Casanova, although egocentric and immature, was a slightly, not a totally peverted and abnormal personality. This cannot be said of another contemporary figure.

Donatien Alphonse François de Sade was born in 1740, being brought up, not by his parents, but by his uncle, the Abbé François de Sade, who openly kept two mistresses, lived at Vaucluse, and was an authority on Petrarch.

Young de Sade married a girl to whom he was not genuinely attracted, being much more interested in her sister. Shortly after his marriage he had his first brush with the law, and was imprisoned at Vincennes for some piece of debauchery, the nature of which, although it caused some considerable scandal at the time, cannot now be discovered.

De Sade, like many other men at this period, kept a *petite maison*—a house, or country cottage maintained purely from erotic motives. This cottage was at Arceuil, near Paris, and already, in 1764, Sade had a worse reputation than most. In that year Police-Inspector Marais wrote a letter to a procuress named la Brissaut, strongly advising her not to provide him with any girls intended to accompany him to Arceuil.

Three years later, some time soon after Easter Day, the scandal known as the 'affaire Keller' broke and the Marquis was for the first time in a really serious position.

Rose Keller, aged thirty-six, stopped the Marquis and begged him for alms as he crossed the Place Ste. Victoire on Easter Day. Sade asked her if she would like to earn some money, she said 'as a housekeeper'. The Marquis claimed later that he told her at the time '*in a partie de libertinage*'. In either case she accepted.

When she arrived at Arceuil, she was taken into a room, 'forced to undress, tied to a bed face downwards, mercilessly beaten several times with whips and sticks, cut about with a knife in numerous places, and had hot sealing wax dropped on her wounds.' She begged her torturer not to kill her because she had not made her Easter confession. Gnashing his teeth he said 'you can confess to *me*!' and attempted to compel her to do so, telling her that he was going to murder her, and bury her in the garden. She refused, however, and finally made her escape, being cared for by a Madame Jouette, from whom the above story was obtained. The evidence must therefore be treated as hearsay, and would not now be accepted by an English court, although, in view of subsequent events in de Sade's life it may with reason be treated as substantially true.

The surgeon called in by the authorities more or less confirmed Jouette's account. De Sade claimed that Keller was a willing victim, and that he had used a martinet, a whip made of knotted cord.

The Marquis' family bought off Keller with the vast sum of 2,400 livres, but the case continued owing to personal rivalries between the persons concerned. In a story which he wrote later, de Sade puts into the mouth of one of the characters the words: 'Recall to the memory of the Paris judges the celebrated incident of 1769, when far more moved to pity by the whipped bottom of a street woman, than by the condition of the common people, whose father they style themselves, yet whom in fact they allow to die of hunger, they determined to accuse a young officer who on his return from the sacrifice of the best years of his life to the welfare of his king, received his reward in the shape of humiliation at the hands of the enemies of the country he had been defending.' In spite of this long and nearly incomprehensible complaint, de Sade in fact obtained a 'letter of abolition' from Louis XV and was acquitted.

The fact that Keller was whipped on Easter Day increased the seriousness of the offence in the eyes of the magistrates, as also it increased the significance of the whole event in the eyes of de Sade.

In 1772 he was once more in trouble, being accused of the attempted poisoning of Marguerite Coste, to whom he was alleged to have given cantharides, a poison and an aphrodisiac. She was severely sick, but never in serious danger, which did not prevent de Sade from being later accused of murder. On the same day he indulged in more complicated activity. He engaged three girls from a brothel and summoned them to a house on the outskirts of the town (Marseilles). Here they were received by the Marquis, beaten by him and then required to beat him. This they were expected to do with an enormous whip 'made of parchment studded with big and little nails and covered with bloodstains.' They refused to use this implement, thinking it too dangerous, and used instead a twig broom, with which they gave him, if it can be believed, eight hundred strokes, which he notched up on the mantelpiece of the room. His valet, who accompanied him on the whole expedition, also whipped him.

He then had anal intercourse with the three girls whilst he himself was treated likewise by his valet. Subsequently he offered the girls sweets, one accepted, and was later taken ill, although not as ill as Marguerite Coste. It will be agreed that his conduct during this incident does not fall into the category of that kind of behaviour generally described as 'sadistic', the phrase coined from his name a century later by Kraft-Ebbing.

Soon after, de Sade and his valet were arrested on charges of sodomy and murder. Of this visit to Marseilles another story is told. (In *Memoirs Secrets* by (?) Dachaumont.)

'The news from Marseilles is that M. le Comte de Sade, who caused such a stir in 1768 by the lunatic horrors which he inflicted on a girl . . . has just provided in this town a spectacle, pleasant at first, but appalling in its consequences. He gave a ball, to which a large number of guests were invited. Into the pudding course he inserted some chocolates so delicious that several people ate them. There were plenty of these, and nobody went short, but in them he had inserted 'Spanish Fly' (cantharides). The virtue of this preparation is well known; and, as it turned out, all those who had eaten it, burning with unchaste desire, gave themselves up to all the excesses to which the most lascivious frenzy can carry one. The ball degenerated into one of those licentious parties renowned among the Romans. The most modest women could not do enough to give expression to the itch which had seized them. Thus M. de Sade enjoyed the sister-in-law with whom he has fled to preserve himself from the penalty which he deserves. Several persons are dead from the excesses to which they gave themselves up in their Priapic fury and others are still severely indisposed.'

In an article published in the *Revue de Paris*, in 1837, another incident alleged to have occurred during the same expedition is described.

'. . . he went to Marseilles some time in the month of June, accompanied by a trusted servant whom he had groomed to assist him in his unspeakable debaucheries. He had provided himself with a supply of chocolates into which had been mixed a strong dose of Spanish Fly, the terrible and dangerous stimulant which causes such frightful disorders of the nervous system. The two accomplices went together to a brothel, where they produced wine, spirits, and the drugged sweets. The effects of the sweets were not confined to laughter, lascivious dances, and the disgusting manifestations of hysteria; one of the unfortunate girls, whom the drug had reduced to the condition of one of the Bacchantes of antiquity, hurled herself out of the window, receiving fatal injuries, whilst the others, half-naked, gave themselves up to the most disgusting debaucheries in full view of a crowd which had assembled in front of the house, which echoed with shrieks and the sound of frenzied singing.

'The Marquis de Sade and his valet had fled, but they were denounced by public opinion, and the magistrates joined with the doctors in establishing the circumstances of this unchaste and criminal plot. Two girls died in consequence of their lascivious frenzy, or perhaps rather of wounds which these unfortunates had inflicted upon themselves in the appalling mêlée.'

Contradictory accounts of all de Sade's escapades followed each incident, and it may well be that here one event has been variously distorted to make several.

De Sade managed to escape serious consequences by fleeing to Italy; and two years later was still occupied in his dubious practices, this time with the assistance and presumed condonation of his wife. In 1777 he was arrested in Paris at the request of his mother, and after a series of arrests and releases, was imprisoned in the Bastille, where he wrote the majority of his obscene, but in large part incomprehensible, works. He became fascinated, like Casanova, with cabalistic pyramids, referring the numerology, in some involved way to the number of strokes given and received at his flagellatory orgies.

The incomprehensibility of much of his literary work is in chief part due to his tortuous and elaborate 'philosophy'. Many people with strong but irrational impulses attempt, chiefly for the sake of their own peace of mind, to explain these by a 'rational' process, the desired conclusion being mistily, but unwaveringly, perceived throughout the argument; and of these people de Sade undoubtedly was one. His argument was of course centred on his unrationalizable sexual impulses, and, although he made a long and probably sincere study of the sexual instinct and its perversions, the degree of his self-delusion is extraordinary.

He was removed, first temporarily, then permanently, to Charenton Lunatic Asylum, where he died in 1814. His desire, expressed in his will, to be buried without ceremony in the middle of a wood, and covered with acorns, was ignored. He was given ordinary Christian burial, although his skull was subsequently dug up and examined by an inquisitive phrenologist who pusillanimously confined his diagnosis to the comment that it indicated 'a mixture of vices and virtues.'

What has caused most horror about the life of the Marquis de Sade is his advocation of the deliberate cultivation of new sexual pleasures. Geoffrey Gorer (*Life and Ideas of the Marquis de Sade*) criticizes this as a reason for condemning him because: 'It is only in the sexual sphere that this is considered reprehensible: in all other human activities the cultivation of a wider taste is held most praiseworthy. The study and development of the arts has no other aim than to enable us to perceive beauty and harmony in shapes, sounds and colours that were before either meaningless or repulsive. An English country parson, who would faint with horror if it were suggested that he and his wife should try to extend in any way their sexual pleasures, will have no hesitation in smearing his child with the bloody tail of a newly-killed fox and encouraging him to enjoy such activity; or in feeding on such stomach-turning delicacies as putrescent game or cheese. And not only will he manage to swallow such naturally revolting food, he will consider it more enjoyable than ordinary nourishment, and will refuse fresh game or cheese as flat and tasteless. "The greatest pleasures are born from conquered repugnances." '

The fallacy in the comparison quoted above (one which de Sade himself was very fond of making) seems to me to be this.

Both rotting birds and their sexual equivalents may taste delicious; but the former have been observed to cause no greater inconvenience than a few hours' indigestion, whilst the latter can be seen to cause permanent damage in the form of misery and a sense of isolation, and would seem to become not something desired and partaken of as a matter of free will, but to possess rather the attraction of a habit-forming and noxious drug. One does no harm: the other can, and usually does, do a good deal more harm than good, if only to the sexual explorer himself. The damage is not always confined to the initiator.

Carrying the argument to its logical extreme, one would arrive at the conclusion that it is admirable to cultivate a taste for the symptoms of Yellow Fever, or a partiality for the odour of Hydrocyanic gas, in order to transcend the essentially limited experiences of conventional but uninspiring health.

'Abnormal' sexual behaviour, although its existence is denied by some, may be defined as behaviour inimicable to life, emotional well-being, and a sense of happiness. The difficulties of recognizing such behaviour are, of course great, and even recognition does not necessarily bring relief. There are many who cling to their diseases and none so fondly as the psychoneurotic brotherhood.

The element of exploration and experimentation involved in abnormal or unusual forms of sexual behaviour is something which needs looking into. It is probably closely connected with the sense of mysticism which many people experience in connexion with sexuality: a feeling, ill-defined that here is another world into which the road to escape, perhaps in the form of self-destruction, lies open.

The unhappy or unsatisfied man, disgusted, and despairing of liberation from his own personality in this world, attempts to abandon himself to what he conceives as control by other forces. Of these forces the mysterious power of his own sexuality seems the most easily available. In his attempt to achieve liberation from responsibility, he usually achieves nothing but further unhappiness and disillusionment, and what appeared at first a means of escape, in fact only contributes further to his sense of confinement.

In England, the word 'romantic' was applicable to literary and artistic movements only. On the Continent it could be used to refer to a whole way of life, or at any rate to an outlook on sexual and married life.

The members of the Continental romantic movement were a minority of easy-going people expressing their loneliness and anarchy among the restrictionists who were, as in England, a steadily increasing force. Their sense of realism, however, was little greater than their opponents.

The Greeks had seen the three functions of woman as: mother, wife, and, not in the derogatory sense, whore. They believed that these were three different women. The romanticist of the eighteenth and nineteenth centuries hoped to find the three qualities incorporated in one girl. Naturally he did not succeed. One of the things one notices about these people is that they did not get anything *done*. They were always searching for the ideal, saving their sexual energies for the great moment when they would achieve the fulfilment of their fantasy: the 'only-girl-in-the-world' fantasy. Perhaps, one uncharitably thinks, they behaved like this because they did not *want* to get anything done.

Some of them effected a compromise in the form of a *mariage à trois*, which must be considered as distinct from the later habit of mistress-keeping. (In the latter case the two establishments were completely apart, in the former the two women lived under the same roof.) Even with this slackening of the rules, the romanticists could not hope long to survive in prototype. We have seen before into what channels a restrictive movement will ultimately divert the sexual instinct. We are to see it again. Even the 'free-thinkers' are not immune from this transformation. The activities of the Medmenham group with their satanic and Gothic fantasies were but the first hint of worse things to come. Sir Francis Dashwood and his associates could enjoy more or less normal sexual activity provided it was dressed up in the right clothes. This was not true of the men and women who were to follow them in an era which was to give birth to such men and women as Princess Belgioso, who kept the embalmed body of her lover in her villa at Locate for several weeks, and would probably have kept it longer, had not a search by the Austrian police revealed her macabre secret. The same lady slept in a bedroom like a catafalque, guarded by a melancholy negro servant, who conducted visitors to her presence with an air of suitable melodrama. Or like Swinburne churning out his dreary necrophilo-sado-masochistic poetry:

> 'But the worm shall revive thee with kisses;
> Thou shalt change and transmute as a god,
> As the rod to a serpent that hisses,
> As the serpent again to a rod.
> Though the heathen outface and outlive us
> And our lives and our longings are twain. . . .
> Ah, forgive us our virtues forgive us.
> Our Lady of Pain.'

This was the poet who was identifying himself by the age of fourteen with characters in the already copious flagellatory pornography which the age produced.

Every kind of elaborate fantasy that the mind could conceive: tortuous, bizarre, ingenious. Every kind of idea, but very little action. These were the trappings of the romanticist as he walked on to the Victorian stage.

SEVEN

THE VICTORIANS

I⊤ has been claimed by a recent author (Cyril Pearl: *The Girl with the Swansdown Seat*), that our ideas about the 'Victorian' period are all wrong. It was not really an age of repression at all. Look at all the prostitutes, humble and magnificent; look at all the scandalous divorce cases, look at all the pornographic literature, the potential suggestiveness of the clothing (the crinolines, the low necklines, the addiction to tighter and tighter corsets) and much more such stuff. It was 'an age when prostitution was widespread and flagrant, when many London streets were like oriental bazaars of flesh . . . when fashionable whores rode with duchesses in Rotten Row.'

Much of what he says is undeniably true, although it is stretching things a little to say that prostitution was 'flagrant' unless one means numerically considerable. Even if this was the case, prostitution on a large scale is a sign either of an age of extreme licence, or of an age of extreme restriction. (Most people do not sleep with whores unless they cannot, or, for one reason or another, do not want to, sleep with anybody else.) Nobody, I hope, will claim the Victorian age as a period of general debauchery, and the presence of prostitution seems to me to fit in very tidily with the rest of the picture as usually visualized by the ordinary man. (Pearl claims that any pigeon-holing of a particular period as restrictive or otherwise is meaningless and probably based on a fallacious system of evidence. I cannot agree. Sex cannot be simply eliminated, it will always be present in one form or another . . . it is the form in which it *does* appear that is interesting, and from which we can fairly make our deductions.)

This criticism applies also to the significance of pornography;

people do not read when they can act . . . unless for some reason or another it has become impossible to extract pleasure from the ordinary forms of sexual behaviour.

The Victorians were strict; but behind the unrealism of their ideals and efforts lay a basic sense of reality. They were severe and idealistic in their aims but they left themselves loopholes. They were not romantics . . . the Victorian habit of mistress-keeping, of getting one's family pleasures in one house and one's sexual in another is sure evidence of that. They had amazingly dirty minds (which, as in the case of the medievals, so far from being incompatible with a period of restriction is the inevitable result of it). They were sometimes wilfully blind, and (always wilfully) illogical.

This dirtiness of their minds was applied to more and more subjects, as more and more topics with indelicate associations were made taboo—both the sexual subjects and the substitutes for them. That the Victorians were possessed of extraordinarily inventive brains to aid them in this replacement is neatly demonstrated by the fairly well-known and very interesting example of the curious incident of the furniture legs.

Victorian gentlemen, as everybody knows, were driven insane with lust by the sight of an accidentally, or perhaps intentionally, exposed female ankle. (Everything else having been covered up, the poor things had to make do with this.) However: some Victorian ladies, projecting on to their male acquaintances their own suppressed unchaste desires, decided that it would be a good thing for their own reputation, the continued preservation of the virtue of their daughters, and the moral welfare of the gentlemen themselves, if the legs of pianos, sofas and armchairs were also encased in clothes resembling those of their female proprietors. In this way there would be no danger that a male visitor might suffer a sudden access of lust at the sight, inevitably accompanied by a simple association of ideas, of a naked 'leg'.

The same sort of thing is to be seen in the maniac expurgating of many completely innocuous books. The propensity for being stimulated by the remotely suggestive with which the editors endowed their readers is truly astounding.

The lines from *As You Like It*:

> Under the greenwood tree
> Who loves to lie with me

in which the verb 'lie' is used in a totally non-sexual sense, a really ludicrous effort of imagination being necessary to make it so; was carefully amended in the Plumtre edition to:

> Under the greenwood tree,
> Who loves to work with me

The real significance of this amendment, which I think is very great, lies in the fact that it ever entered Plumtre's head that anyone might twist the passage into, let alone originally read it in, the sense in which he himself obviously interpreted it. This significance is increased when one reflects that his fear was undoubtedly well founded.

The same obsession was to be seen in the case of the spoken word (the male domestic fowl being referred to by the polite as a 'rooster'), and in the changing of surnames which seemed to the sensitive ear of their possessors to be indelicate.

The practical agent of the restrictive movement was, of course, the paterfamilias, who was probably able to add a financial, as well as a moral hold on the behaviour of his wife and offspring.

How, in practice, did the average man and woman react to this situation? There can be very little doubt, in the case of girls of the upper and middle classes, that, before marriage, they had in the vast majority of cases, no relief except masturbation (if they had been left with the gumption to practice even this). This was due, quite apart from any question of mental repugnance, caused by more or less deliberate psychological indoctrination, to physical impractibility.

In the case of young men (we will return to the married

of both sexes presently), the chances, presuming adequate strength of character, were none too bad.

The prostitute population of London at this period was adequate in number and easily accessible. Even the psychological restraints were not too severe, or at any rate not comparable with those affecting their sisters. The differences between the moral code in theory, and the same in practice is always considerable. The Victorians would continue to *say* that men should be chaste before marriage, and having said so, they could, with a clearer conscience, encourage their sons, though not of course in so many words, to go whoring round the town improving their sexual education.

Not all the Victorians, or, at base, the Press, deluded themselves with this little piece of schizophrenia.

Contemporary newspapers contain, as might be expected, a large number of letters demanding the systematic cleansing of the streets. They also contain replies defending the right of the tart to ply for trade—although the writers of such letters are usually insincere about their motives and insert a strong lacing of sentimentality, basing their arguments on the principles of Christian tolerance and charity and the alleged 'pathetic' and 'defenceless' condition of the ladies in question. (The fact that some, at least, of them had incomes larger than their defenders was absolutely ignored.)

In 1841 the population of the area now known as Greater London, was 2,235,344. In 1857 there were, on the estimate of *The Lancet*, 80,000 prostitutes in London (County). In 1951 there were believed to be 10,000. These estimates probably include part-times and semi-amateurs, but exclude, one presumes, some whores of the courtesan variety. *The Lancet* also claims that out of any sixty houses, one at least was a brothel, and out of any sixteen women (of all ages!), one a prostitute. These figures are of course, although copied from and by other 'investigators', absolutely unreliable. They were believed at the time, but this tells us more about the attackers than the attacked.

It is true that the figures given by *The Lancet* conform more or less with those of Michael Ryan, a medical man, if he deserves the name, of the 1830s, but then as likely as not they were based on them. Mayhew's estimate of *c.* 7,000 seems much more likely (even he was later led into wilder statements, the mystical figure 80,000 displaying an irresistible attraction). Ryan's book displays throughout a complete inability to distinguish fact from fiction.

Although medically qualified, he states as a scientific fact that masturbation has been proved to result in diseases such as 'the worst form of hypochondriasis—aneurism—all the diseases of the brain and spinal marrow, feebleness of the whole muscular system, chronic inflammation of the viscera of the chest, abdomen and pelvis—consumption, stricture of the uretha—incontinence of urine, piles, nocturnal emissions, etc., etc.'

From this wild and implausible list some inkling of the reliability of this authority may be gleaned. He is merely concerned to make out a case in accordance with his emotional beliefs.

If the figures of *The Lancet* are correct, and assuming that these girls averaged fifteen customers a week (certainly an underestimate), it would mean, as Pearl, although he plumps for the more exciting figure, has pointed out, that between them they would have received weekly a number of men noticeably larger than the entire male population of London (including, in accordance with the statistical practice of the period, 'babes in arms'). Something seems to have gone wrong somewhere with somebody's arithmetic. But even if one accepts the lower figure the basic contradiction remains.

Country clergymen might complain that they had been roughly seized by the arm in the Haymarket, and accosted in a variety of Romance languages, by a number of women many of whom were drunk and some of whom were smoking cigars. Respectable residents might complain of the noises of carousal and laughter. The committees might collect, or, rather concoct, their statistics and present their horrified reports. The shopkeepers of Regent Street might be willing to pull down the beautiful Nash pillars, which had been standing only thirty-five years, in order to conform with the pretensions of their customers and spite the ladies of the town who gathered in their shadow at night. The Press might seize the opportunity for a little 'exposure of these appalling conditions' in order to boost their sales for a week or two. But somebody was patronizing these ladies. Who?

There is no doubt who the majority of the ladies themselves were. They were members of the lower classes, factory girls and other underpaid females, who could not afford the delicate moral scruples of their betters, and who knew well enough that the males of the species would not hesitate to summon them to their relief.

The factories of the nineteenth century got the blame for sexual immorality in much the same way that 'broken homes' and other psychological causes are blamed for every act of juvenile delinquency today. It was claimed, possibly with justification, that the intense heat to which the girls were subjected during their long working hours, aroused in them a premature and unnatural degree of lust, which the young gentlemen of the neighbourhood gave them every opportunity of satisfying.

These villains, one reforming zealot claimed, took houses in the neighbourhood 'to which their victims repaired, nothing loth, to share the disgraceful orgies of their paramours.' At these, says Mr. Gaskell—the writer in question—'scenes were enacted that even put to the blush the lascivious saturnalia of the Romans, the rites of the Pagoda girls of India, and the harem life of the most voluptuous Ottoman.'

Mr. Gaskell's imagination has clearly been running away with him, how far it is difficult with certainty to guess. If his facts are more or less accurate, the source of the supply to the Metropolis is explained. The age of consent being, at this period, twelve years of age, any girl so minded would be able, having once savoured the sweet taste of easy money, to embark all the earlier on her long and profitable career.

The prostitute was the scapegoat of the nineteenth century, and the Victorians used her to carry their lusts for them, just as the Medieval Church had loaded all the sins of the world on the heads of the witches.

To some she appeared as a monster, to others as a martyr, to others angels of mercy. Perhaps the most common view of her was as somebody who, having sucked the poison out of another's system becomes, although a heroine, poisonous and untouchable.

But what, in fact, was the nature of the escape they offered, these ladies of theoretically low, but in fact high repute?

The most conspicuous form in which prostitution appeared, and that which aroused the most frenzied blasts of crusading zeal on the part of the puritanical, was the presence of numerous whores, how numerous has already been discussed, blocking up the street with their tent-like crinolines, bringing blushes to the cheeks of the prudish and the pretentious, and making passage difficult to all and sundry. There were even during the first years of Victoria's reign, still a few of the 'theatre whores' whom we met in the previous chapter; but these were in a minority, and although, rather curiously, what most attracted the displeasure of the general and respectable theatre-going public was not their profession, but because 'they do not dress respectably', they were regarded as distinctly second-rate by their business associates.

Many of these had only a dubious right to sneer, but even those in the upper ranks, the brothel-dwelling class, were not immune from *public* displeasure. The blockage of the Haymarket, of Regent Street, and of the Burlington Arcade might cause outcry, so also did the conditions in some other streets in the West End, whether the night-life of London had been steadily and stealthily crawling.

Norton Street, it would appear, was almost solid whorehouse from end to end. The denizens of the various establishments made the street impassable to the chaste by their habit of sitting naked on the window-sills and of rushing out into the street in their underclothes to drag unwilling gentlemen in to what, the crusaders implied, was practically a rape.

Maybe the accounts have been a little exaggerated, as they always have been and always will be. None the less, conditions were gay enough if you knew where to look.

In the eighteen-fifties there was flourishing, off Leicester Square, a fashionable and luxuriously furnished 'saloon' based on the American pattern. At this establishment, once you had gained admission to it, for this was not available to all—it was possible to obtain a large variety of that then fantastically daring innovation—the cocktail. The aura of rarity and vulgarity surrounding this drink made its consumption an act that in itself marked one as a blood of the first category, even if one did nothing else. This was an unlikely event.

At the end of the room the proprietress of this establishment, Kate Hamilton, sat glittering with jewels, not all of them paste, upon a velvet throne. She was attended by a corps of young and beautiful ladies-in-waiting, to whom she issued commands in her loud and scarifyingly harsh voice. Ugly and fat, she was a woman to be frightened of, and indeed with good reason, for she enjoyed a reputation as absolute monarch of her little kingdom, and was highly particular as to who came down the subterranean passage which led to her dominions. Not only were the customers carefully scrutinized through a peep-hole in the door: it was a smart tart who came up to Kate's requirements and was allowed to fill her purse from the aristocratic pockets of the assembled company. There were many eager to do so, and those who did come did not go anywhere else. 'They would shrink from appearing at any of the cafés in the Haymarket, or at the supper rooms in which the adjacent streets abound,' said Mayhew.

Even Royalty patronized her saloon on occasion. In 1857 she had the honour of receiving a visit from the two kings of Siam (there were two at this time for some reason or another) accompanied by the Siamese ambassador. Although they sampled only the beverages of the place they seem to have gone down very well, possibly on account of their habit of standing drinks all round, and their general lack of stand-offishness.

The Shah of Persia, he who received a rather chilly reception at Buckingham Palace, owing to his uninhibited table manners and the rather too unambiguous manner in which he indicated his approval of the physical charms of a lady-in-waiting; also paid a visit, although, if Mr. Beeton can be believed, of a different, more furtive, and less popular kind.

In Beeton's *Christmas Annual* for 1873 there appeared an immense epic poem, *The Siliad* dealing, among other follies and abuses, with the night-life of the town.

After scrutinizing the women of the Haymarket:

> '. . . where vice
> Imparts the tariff and proclaims the price.
> Her stocks are quoted; some at premium stand;
> And "French" are lively, and in great demand:
> "Belgians" are sluggish, though there is no lack:
> The trade in "Africans" is rather slack:
> Of "British" high and low the prices range,
> Although the top quotations show no change.'

They move on to Kate's where the prices are more unpredictable. However, she seems glad to see them, and they to see her, for they greet her in rapturous adoration:

> 'O buxom woman, handsome in thy day,
> Whose gay career the police courts cannot stay.'

Perhaps in gratitude at this flattering and suitably deferential address, she allows them to withdraw to one of the private rooms. On the way, one of the party blunders into the wrong room, and, oh horrors, what is this?

> 'What face is that, as dusky as the night,
> That jewelled form, those cruel, wicked eyes,
> That sparkle savagely at this surprise?'

"It is the Shah!" a voice cries in the gloom.'

And, as it soon turned out:

'It *was* the Shah; the wily potentate,
Was studying the secrets of our state,
Which three fat actresses with might and main,
Had been in turn endeavouring to explain.'

However, although they consider the Shah:

'A cruel Eastern Sensualist at best,
Unfit for widowed queen as honoured guest,'

they tactfully withdraw, leaving him to his diversions, and go to
their own room, where:

'. . . till the advent of the supper-tray,
They worship Venus in a quiet way.'

Stupified, they gaze around them at the sumptuosity of
the décor which, they feel:

'. . . invites
To thorough worship and elaborate rites:
The ceiling glass, tall mirrors line the walls,
Beneath the footsteps on pile velvet falls,
Three satin-covered couches . . . one sky-blue,
And one coal-black, and one rich crimson's hue.
The pictures all one sentiment suppress;
'Tis female loveliness unmarred by dress.'

Their train of thought is broken, or at any rate temporarily
diverted, by the entry of a gargantuan meal.

'Insular "natives",' lobsters, a capon, ox-tongue, fowl à la
mayonnaise, vol-au-vent, 'tomatoes cooked two ways', a
frickassee of chickens, lamb and peas, devilled kidneys, a

snowy trifle ('volatile as air'), ice-cream, meringue, tipsy-cake, charlotte-aux-pommes, Crème de Noyeau, all washed down by quantities of champagne, and Curacoa-and-soda in silver goblets. After, presumably, several hours of unbroken eating, a line of asterisks appears, after which the bill is, with some trepidation, called for:

> '. . . O muse be dumb,
> nor fright us with a mention of its sum,'

they pusillanimously and unrealistically exclaim.

But, as it turns out, the evening's fun is not yet over, for they have a good gossip with Kate. Unfortunately the subject-matter cannot be repeated, for:

> '. . . Kate's had been the trusted trysting-place
> Of many nobs who did not go the pace,
> Confessedly . . . yet seeming solemn prigs,
> Were secretly extremely fond of "rigs".'

Stimulated by the information they receive, they gain fresh wind, and call for an extension of the evening.

> 'Hebes, this time in lowly disarray,
> Bring odorous Mocha on a silver tray:
> And, staying now and then to toy and pet,
> With deftness roll the fragrant cigarette.
> The weeds they light, on Nicotina call
> And dreamy ecstasy comes down on all;
> With what haps next not ours it is to deal
> For clouds of smoke ascend, and all conceal.'

In the small hours they are awakened from an exhausted sleep by the 'noise of trampling feet' which, as they rightly surmise, indicates a raid by the police. Here a flaw in the otherwise perfect arrangement is brought to light, for, in answer to their anxious inquiries Kate tells them, with remarkable unconcern, that her establishment has 'no back doors'.

They see that it is necessary to fight their way out, and after organizing a resistance movement they succeed in accomplishing this, inflicting heavy losses in blood and equipment on the invading officers, subsequently regaling themselves at the club with sal-volatile and 'floods of wine'.

When the business changed hands after Kate's death, it fell on evil days of police interference. A police-inspector who raided the premises claimed that the whores outnumbered the gentlemen by 95–90—a sign of the true purpose for which most males attended. However, later, in evidence, the same inspector reported that he had said to William Barton, the new proprietor: 'You have more than seventy prostitutes here.' Barton retorted with admirable spirit and presence of mind: 'It does not matter if there are one hundred and fifty if they conduct themselves in an orderly fashion.' During the hearing, the gentleman living opposite stated that his nights were disturbed by the constant arrival of tarts in cabs, some unaccompanied, some with gentlemen, all of them making a considerable din and offending his sense of decency.

Barton got off with a £3 fine, which even in those days, when money was money, cannot have seriously incommoded him.

Not all of the establishments of this kind were run with such decorum. It was, according to the police, and to a certain extent, to their records, a period of singular insobriety and rowdiness.

Free entertainment of, for the Victorians, a high degree of indecency was provided by the divorce trials. These were open to all members of the public lucky enough to be able to squeeze themselves into the public galleries. Evidence of a highly indecent nature was given; and avidly listened to by those who publicly lamented the necessity for pure young maidservants to give, blushing, details of what they had, inadvertently, observed through keyholes. Privately, it need hardly be said, they extracted every ounce of satisfaction from the case, noting for purposes of future private reference, and meditation, how holes had been bored in the wall, how stains had been found in the bed, the nature of the noises that had emerged from the room.

The Victorians, more than any other people at any period of history, had to learn to take their sexual pleasures vicariously. The system had its disadvantages. Such pleasures were marred for the audiences by the mask of sanctity and horror which they were compelled to wear.

However, the pleasure was one that needed looking into—if there was not enough real immorality it was always possible to substitute make-believe.

Make-believe escape from the conventions was provided by the enterprising 'Baron' Renton Nicholson, who held improved encores of recent cases, supplementing them with additions of his own. The court, says Greville, who thought the proceedings 'disgusting'—'deals in very gross obscenities'.

'Baron' Nicholson had had a chequered career; in his youth he had earned a living as a pawnbroker, and by running a roulette wheel in a tent on a racecourse. Before he died he published his memoirs, on the title-page of which appeared a bogus coat-of-arms with the motto '*Ecce incorporo hilaritatem cum lege.*' The memoirs, although written with a good deal of rather hypocritical sentimentality, contain much interesting material about the Baron and his early acquaintances— prize-fighters, criminals, whores and panders. But it was his court which brought him real fame and money, the success being doubled as he himself remarks, when in 1846 he introduced his 'poses plastiques'. These consisted of the presentation, in tight costumes of flesh-coloured silk, of various delightful ladies carefully posed on a revolving stage, which was worked by hand to the accompaniment of much un-oiled squeaking, and the breathless grunts of the operators.

During his lifetime, the Baron, with a long life of bitter experience behind him, pursued his trade with success and in peace. His clientele were considered, apart from the fact that they were present at his entertainments at all, to be respectable; and he evaded, at any rate in connexion with his court, any serious brush with the established law. Over his distinguished customers he appears to have exercised a magnetic fascination, for they always addressed him by his assumed title, treating him in other ways with every mark of respect.

His successor was too ambitious and less well connected, being soon brought before the magistrates charged with presenting an obscene performance. So was another imitator with a court at Hampstead, although it was generally agreed that his wit was not so great.

So far, the public facilities for sexual indulgence dealt with have all been for the satisfying of more or less normal sexual desires. But the morality campaigns and the hypocritical conventions could not fail to leave their mark on some.

There were those to whom the knowledge that they were tasting forbidden fruit would bring an extra pleasure, a superior thrill as they passed down the subterranean passage leading to Kate's abode of bliss. These were the anarchists, the men with the strong personalities on whom the conventions of the age left no mark other than reaction.

Not all were so lightly affected. The proportion of the brothels dealing with perversions (in particular the three obsessions of the previous century already catalogued), remained alarmingly high.

Outstanding amongst these manifestations was the increasing demand for young girls and virgins. Wickham Steed dealt with this traffic at length during his editorship of the *Pall Mall Gazette*. At first he was extremely unpopular, and by many absolutely disbelieved, but finally he obtained the commission of inquiry for which he had been yammering.

A 'scandalous system of procuration' was exposed. Since factory girls had usually lost all semblance of virginity long before they reached London, it was necessary to search elsewhere. Nursemaids were accosted in the park, hunting expeditions made to the country. More horrifying, it was discovered that aged members of the profession were selling (literally selling as slaves) the illegitimate female produce of their activities for comparatively low sums. In some cases, it was alleged, the girls were sold for exportation overseas.

In spite of a sudden surge of feeling in favour of Steed—whose supporters staged an enormous parade round Hyde Park in which the marchers wore white roses as a sign of their purity (the effect only being marred by an escort of prostitutes soliciting trade)—nothing was done. Lip-service was the motto of the Victorians and would remain so.

The strain imposed by the degree of sexual continence required by conventional morality, would, had he attempted to practise it, have killed any normal man. It simply is not in the nature of human beings, nor is it physically practicable for them to be completely abstinent. The young man of the nineteenth century might attempt to solve his problems by marriage. Even this would be unlikely to prove completely effective. In fact, of course, he did not practise abstinence. All that the Victorians really practised was hypocrisy, and the kind of controlled schizophrenia we have already seen. Even the strain of this was too great. In fact, in particular the strain of this. The reaction was sudden and violent.

In 1867 *London Society* wrote: 'Not many years ago, it would have been considered the very acme of indecency and impudence . . . for any young man . . . to appear even to notice in public' (N.B. 'in public') 'any of these "fair unfortunates" ' . . . 'such regard for the proprieties of life scarcely remains.'

It did not indeed. Suddenly the ladies of the town, the better known of them, became visible to respectable eyes. Not only visible, but approachable. A young man, out riding or walking in the park with his sister, felt no inhibitions about raising his hat or speaking to a lady known by everybody to be a courtesan. And his sister would not mind. Far from it. Immorality had become smart. It actually became the ambition of many young ladies of perfectly respectable family and habits, to dress as, behave as, and possibly even to be mistaken for a tart. They did not, of course wish this misapprehension to be carried to its logical conclusion. They had not yet the nerve to make their dreams real. But all the same. . . .

The "smart set" at any given period has always tried to set itself unmistakably apart from the rest of society; to show that it is different—to rebel. Rebellion is the essence of the orgy; rebellion against the accepted standards. It may be temporary. It may be permanent. If it is a permanent movement it still cannot avoid passing through a period of transition, during which it remains a recognized exception instead of the rule.

This minority movement, in the present instance, in the case of a few individuals has been continuous.

There were alive, at this period of the harlot's return to respectability, plenty of men who could remember old Lord Hertford, who, said Greville:

'When between sixty and seventy years old, broken with various infirmities, and almost unintelligible from a paralysis of the tongue . . . had been in the habit of travelling about with a company of prostitutes, who formed his principle society, and by whom he was surrounded up to the moment of his death; generally picking them up from the dregs of that class and changing them according to his fancy and caprice. Here he was to be seen driving about the town, and lifted by two footmen from the carriage into the brothel . . . he never seems to have thought it necessary to throw the slightest veil over the habits he pursued.'

These days were fast returning, and with them the reign of the fashionable courtesan. The tarts ceased to be an invisible anonymity, and began to be known by name—even if this was assumed. Cora Pearl, Skittles, Mabel Gray, Laura Bell, Kate Cook, Agnes Willoughby, and many others.

The most remarkable of these ladies, English-born, although she spent much of her life on the Continent, was Cora Pearl. Born in Devonshire as Emma Elizabeth Crouch, she soon saw, if no one else did, the potentialities of her head of red hair and her sexy little cat's face. She decided on her profession, and that she was going to rise to the top of it.

Methodically she ascended the ladder of whoredom. Her life, although she did not know it, was to be a short one. She wasted no time. Avaricious, original and inventive she 'was able to keep in the front rank because of her inordinate talent for voluptuous eccentricities.' She gave parties at which the guests were perpetually on edge. What would Cora do next? Several times she made her appearance on, not at, the dinner-table, being served up naked with the comestibles on, or rather under, a large silver-covered dish. Once, when the cover was raised she was encased in sauce, anticipating the games of transatlantic millionaires half a century later. She danced the *cancan* on a floor carpeted with roses, and bathed before all her guests in a silver tub filled with champagne. The constant organizer of rowdy parties, she was expelled, at one time or another, by the police of Baden, Monte Carlo, Nice, Vichy, and Rome. Before writing her memoirs she communicated with all her lovers inquiring how much they would be prepared to pay to be omitted from the contents. This must have proved a profitable enterprise, for the resulting work is startlingly uninteresting. Although an original, she was not a pleasant woman, apart from her cupidity the twanging cockney accent in which she uttered the obscenities which were the stock-in-trade, rather than the unavoidable inheritance of the nineteenth-century courtesan, added to the impression of harshness and insensitivity.

Strongly narcissistic, she had had constructed a plaster of Paris cast of her breasts, and this curious object was found amongst other junk in the Paris garret where she died of cancer and in poverty in 1886.

The admirers of the various ladies of the town were not confined to those lucky enough to be in possession of the funds necessary for enjoying them. Those who could not afford actual relief from the restraints imposed on them by convention obtained it vicariously. Photographs of the ladies were displayed in the windows of tobacconists of a certain type, and labelled with their names; for they enjoyed a renown equal to, and enjoyed a worship more intense than any film star of the twentieth century. They were worshipped almost with the devotion bestowed upon Venus and Aphrodite, and their inaccessibility made them not only more desirable, but more unreal and god-like.

A few of the admirers who were close to them did in fact contract marriages with them, but such marriages were never a success. Henry Vane Milbank was only restrained by the violent and determined intervention of his relations from contracting such a marriage; and William Frederick Windham actually did so. His marriage with Agnes Willoughby resulted in an attempt to restrain his actions by means of a Commission in Lunacy. He had in fact been known as 'mad' Windham when at Eton, although this was no great evidence of insanity. It was also claimed that he was fond of dressing up in the uniforms of policemen and railway-porters, of imitating cats, chickens and other animals, of screaming hysterically, and of eating as many as seventeen eggs for breakfast. The attempt to declare him insane was a failure, and he received a terrific public ovation; but his marriage with Agnes Willoughby was on the rocks in less than two months. This was perhaps not surprising. He made her an allowance of only £800 a year and she could earn considerably more by other means. The true moral of the story is that the whole point of the nineteenth-century tart was that she was a tart, and that she remains in part mysterious and inaccessible.

The real disease of the Victorians, as also the reason why the males resorted to prostitutes for their sexual satisfaction rather than to their own wives, was a kind of retention of the emotions, a deliberate self-anaesthesia. When the Victorian gentleman was having sexual relations with his wife, she, if not he, had to withhold from themselves the realization that they were experiencing pleasure. That this was obviously profoundly emotionally unhealthy for both of them is a fact that does not need stating. Every human being needs an occasional emotional purge, just as he feels, from time to time, the need to defecate or vomit. It seems likely that the Victorians had some idea of this and that they attempted to drain the sexuality from their systems in some suitably disguised form.

The schoolmastering profession have not been famous for their self-insight or for progressiveness in sexual matters. In the nineteenth century, games became both organized and universal in the public schools of England. Athletes are well known not to be possessed of a powerful sex drive. This urge, if it cannot come out under its true colours, will appear in other forms. I am not suggesting that the reason behind the enjoyment of games is purely, or even in major part, a sexual one. I am suggesting that, in the case of schoolboys at the age of puberty—the peak point of their sexual desires—much of the excitement connected with the playing of games has this origin. As a substitute for sexual activity it has the advantage of providing opportunity to demonstrate aggressive power and superiority over others. One of the factors that confirms me in this suspicion is, I freely confess, the fact that the Victorians were at such pains to sponsor the playing of games in schools.

However, one should look for an outlet more consciously cathartic than any yet discovered, although considering the nature of the spirit of age, one should not expect necessarily to find it. One of the aspects of social life which, as we by now know, must always be examined in this connexion, is the dance.

Dancing in this period is usually conceived of as being rather stately and formal, fraught, in fact, with every kind of impediment to spontaneous behaviour. This may have been true of society dances, it was not true of others. The dance that I have in mind, and which instantly attracts our attention is the *cancan*. This dance is, by some, now conceived as a rather *démodé* type of music-hall entertainment—pretty tame stuff— and so it may be. It was not always so.

It should be remembered that women did not normally show their legs above the ankle. The imagination might roam higher, but not the eyes. The *cancan* remedied this displaying besides other very startling features.

It had been popular on the Continent for some years, first as a social dance—'a rather rowdy social dance', says the *Dance Encyclopaedia*, and then as a theatrical entertainment.

It was staged in the latter form in England in 1867 and in spite of, or perhaps as *The Times* pretended to think, because of, the modification of some of the more blatant indecencies, was an instant success.

In Paris, when it first appeared in the 1830s it caused first displeasure, then active interference on the part of the police. Apart from the rather obvious significance of some of the movements, it was believed by some to have a political significance, as, in a sense, it had.

Kracauer says that it was used by the revolutionary and anarchic-minded to indicate their anger and contempt for the new régime, and for the rest of society.

Another observer of the *cancan*, quoted by Pearl says:

'The beat of the music is hastened, the dancers' movements become more rapid, more animated, more aggressive, and finally the contredanse evolves into a great gallop. . . . Though at this stage individual indecent movements are no longer seen, the dancers' behaviour and facial expression bear witness to a more intense voluptuousness . . . for the music gets quicker and quicker, until one finally sees masked women, like ecstatic maenads, with flushed cheeks, breathless heaving breasts, parched lips, and half-undone flying hair, careering round the room, less on their feet than being dragged along bodily.'

The emotions of Europe were being let loose and once they had scented the odour of freedom nothing could stop them. This change may have been aided in England by the snob-value bestowed on immorality by the activities of the Prince of Wales, soon to be Edward VII. When the mistress of a dying king could be summoned to the death-bed, it could no longer be concealed that times had changed.

The process was completed by the upheaval of Society

during the First World War. Completed is, unfortunately, the wrong word.

People never learn by their own mistakes, still less by the mistakes of others. Those who remembered or felt the presence of Victorian repression with displeasure, attempted to escape from the memory, not realizing that not only conventions but the lack of them can make a cage.

If claustrophobia of the spirit had been the disease of the Victorians, agoraphobia of the spirit was to torment their grandchildren.

EIGHT

THE TWENTIETH CENTURY

THERE cannot be many who would hesitate before admitting that the present age is, in the sexual sense, a period of freedom. Even ignoring the gap between theoretical and actual morality which is always present—an examination of the theoretical giving an impression of a stricter code of morality than that which actually prevails—this would appear an indisputable fact.

Moreover; the swing towards liberty has not yet reached its ultimate point. Various active trends suggest this: concern about the laws affecting homosexuals and prostitutes; concern of a kind very different from the nineteenth-century type; attempts to repeal or emasculate the Obscene Publications Act.

There are still those who oppose these movements, and, as in previous periods, they make a degree of noise disproportionate to their true number. In this they are now aided by the press, whose influence on public thought is now much greater than those of the ancient churches (in England at any rate), and whose motives do considerably less to excuse them.

But abuse of those resisting the present liberalizing movements cannot conceal the fact that the experiment has not so far been a complete success even though the extreme limits of licence, such as were displayed during the Renaissance, have not been reached.

That many of the citizens of the twentieth century suffer from a common malaise is, alas, only too plain to be seen. What one should consider is how far this malaise is directly connected with or caused by the 'new morality'.

I believe that the two are very closely connected; although

they are not necessarily cause and effect. This belief is, in its initial conception, based on instinct rather than on a rational process. This is not to say that it cannot be confirmed by such a process, dangerous though this system may be.

There is a tendency, very wide-spread but unjustifiable, to ascribe all human ills to external rather than to internal circumstances. It is believed that every inconvenience is due to something or other, and that if this cause can be detected and eliminated, the inconvenience will cease.

Human beings have become intoxicated with their own performance in the field of scientific discovery, but have proved quite unable to apply the same skill, lack of prejudice, and care, in using their investigatory methods on themselves. When they attempt to do so, something invariably goes wrong.

The swing from restriction to liberty illustrates this as well as anything. People who are miserable, who feel dissatisfaction and lack of fulfilment, sometimes attribute these afflictions to the nature of the social system in which they live. Their belief infects others. There is a change from restrictive to liberal or vice versa. But do their feelings of dissatisfaction disappear? In the present case they have not.

The situation would be a good deal simpler if the belief that the society is to blame was absolutely unjustified. But it is not. Far from it. And yet, when the cause of the trouble is removed, the trouble remains. Why? Is dissatisfaction a human need; a substance which will always be present, directed against one cause or another, if one is removed re-directing itself against others? It seems strange that it should be so, but there also seems, on consideration, good reason for believing that it may be. Little advantage is to be gained from pondering the question 'why?' however interesting the process. Human beings are as yet unable to examine their own insides through a steady microscope. They seem even more unable, unlike most other animals, unlike even vegetables, to distinguish particular actions and general courses of behaviour which are conducive towards, from those which are inimicable to a sane and satisfactory life. A period of balance is more likely to produce a contented body of men than any other, yet how often has there been such a period, and when there has been, how long has it endured? The human race has hurtled through such midway positions with the speed of an express train contemptuously passing through a wayside station on its journey from one capital to another.

The men and women of this century do not suffer from restriction of their movements by actual external impedimenta. They do not suffer many of the more serious consequences induced in the citizens of a restrictive society by subconscious mental processes. Yet they suffer.

However many locks are undone, human beings remain imprisoned in their several cages. Twentieth-century man is no freer than his nineteenth-century predecessor. At least, one assumes that he cannot *feel* free, for everywhere he is making frantic efforts to escape from . . . something. This something he has been unable to identify, but its existence is necessary to his peace of mind: if there is no cause to be destroyed, how then can he escape the result? Everywhere he is still indulging in excesses of drink, food, violence, and copulation; he is attempting to use the ancient system of orgy, but he cannot succeed in his attempts at purging himself, because he does not know of what it is that he wishes to be purged.

The purging action is but one feature of the orgy, the theoleptic aspect is the other. Human beings are *not* rational, in fact they appear unwilling in the extreme to part from their irrationalities. Tired of the attempt to balance their primitive and 'civilized' tendencies; more and more frightened for the safety of the former by the encroachments of the latter, it is not surprising if some of them turn, shuddering, from the vistas spread before them by the increase in scientific knowledge and attempt to regain the mysticism of the ancients.

They project themselves back to a time when at least *everything* was incomprehensible. It is the twilight of knowledge which produces unendurable fidgetiness in men.

This attempt to put back the clock appears for the most part in minor ways. The loving hoarding of little superstitions safe from the scientists, which, instead of being a source of primitive dread induce now just the reverse, a feeling of security in those who practise them. But those who carry these ideas further tend to be regarded as not mistaken, but as frauds.

Sir Francis Dashwood did not *really* believe in the satanistic mumbo jumbo with which he dolled up his basically sexual indulgences. He lived in the middle of the eighteenth century. Yet a man born over a hundred years after Dashwood's death carried the sincerity and devoutness of his belief in a similar creed to far greater lengths than anything of its kind which had attracted general notice since the middle ages.

Edward Alexander Crowley, apart from being a unique character in himself, possesses, as a subject for study, the added, and only just not incompatible attraction, of displaying in interesting olla podrida, the blended characteristics of several of our previous acquaintances.

The son of a prominent and energetic member of the Plymouth Brethren, he was obsessed, like his father, with the idea of sin, although it manifested itself within his personality in a rather different and unorthodox form. With early aspirations towards poetry, he modelled himself at first on Swinburne:

> 'All degradation, all sheer infamy,
> Thou shalt endure, thy head beneath the mire,
> And dung of worthless women shall desire,'

wrote the undergraduate Crowley, who had already decided to change his first name to Aleister as being more magically propitious.

His mystical attitude to life was early formed, if not congenital, and he combined this with a consciousness of, or rather a belief in, his own hermaphroditism and a display of masochistic tendencies. He appears to have thought of himself as surrendering his mind and person to the powers of nature and to the powers of lust and cruelty, to let them lead him whither they would, revealing to him by their commands, the will of the Pantheistic deity whose existence his beliefs implied. In later life the same idea was still obsessing him, though in a changed and modified form.

This mystical attitude he displayed when, in writing of an incident in which he unluckily caught gonorrhoea from a prostitute in Glasgow, he says, apparently with perfect seriousness, that he was 'handed over bound and blindfold to the outraged majesty of Nature.'

An element of masochism cannot be absent from any theoleptic process.

At this early period of his life Crowley could not decide whether the 'presence' of which he had become aware through these ancient mediums of worship, was good or evil. He inclined perhaps towards the latter theory; perhaps towards neither, for the god in whom he really believed was Pan. To achieve communion with his presence he used, besides narcotics, a system of 'sex-magic' or, to put it plainly, copulation. He was undoubtedly an oversexed man, but he was equally undoubtedly sincere in his beliefs, and his motives must, for practical purposes, be treated as religious ones. His unceasing search for the 'right' woman can be interpreted as indicating an insatiable desire for yet more deeply satisfying sexual experiences, but Crowley would interpret such promiscuousness as a means of achieving the best possible understanding of the 'presence' from whom he was to discover the nature of his 'true will'. He regarded women essentially as a means to an end, giving it as his opinion on more than one occasion, that they should be 'brought round to the back door, like milk.' Undoubtedly he had a very good opinion of himself. Was he not the chosen recipient of the information which the 'presence' had decided to communicate via him, Aleister Crowley, to mankind?

His attempts to establish contact with the deities seem to have been remarkably successful even without the use of 'sex-magic'. His 'Book of the Law' was dictated to him word for word at the rate of one chapter a day by Aiwass 'the Holy Guardian Angel'. He met the spirit by appointment, taking down the words of wisdom as fast as he could scribble. The book was published under his own name.

His proselytizing zeal eventually led to the formation of an organization known as The Brothers and Sisters of the A∴ A∴ .

About the same time, he wrote seven 'rites' which were publicly performed at Caxton Hall. These seem to have been incomprehensible rather than indecent, and they received for the most part very unfavourable reviews. During his leadership of the Brothers and Sisters, Crowley became more and more interested in 'sexual magic' as a means of communication with the unseen. At this time he began to wear a kind of phallic hair-style, shaving his head completely bald save for one lock in the centre of his brow. His meeting with the leader of another society holding very similar views—the 'Ordo Templis Orientis' helped to confirm him in this line of experiment.

His activities at this period were described by the *World Magazine*, whose reporter claimed to have attended a ceremony in the Fulham Road where, in a room 'fitted up with divans, and literally carpeted with cushions' the mysteries of The Beast and his followers were supposed to take place. 'Chinese-like' music, sinister-looking books bound in black leather, and cabalistic signs painted on the floor, contributed to the impression of corruption and unreality. A tortured golden snake writhed across the altar. The worshippers entered. Many were 'women of aristocratic type.' The ladies were masked, the portions of their faces which were visible seeming 'as white as wax.' The priests chanted, the candles flickered and went out; 'unspeakable orgies followed.'

Apparently by no means dismayed at this description of his activities, Crowley departed at the commencement of the 1914 war for the United States.

Still rather Swinburnian in his attitude towards women, he worked his way through a series of exotic and deformed mistresses. On these he wrote brief but pungent comments. 'Claims to be "pure American" (!) but is, I think, a mixture of Negro and Japanese.' And: 'big fat negress, very passionate.'

He also advertised for: 'Dwarfs, hunchbacks, tattooed women . . . freaks of all sorts, colored women only if exceptionally ugly or deformed.'

In the United States he met his first 'Scarlet Woman'— Leah Faesi, a Swiss-born American of striking rather than attractive appearance, with whom he appears to have fallen immediately in love, as she with him.

Whilst in America, he wrote his Hymn to Pan: one of his more successful poems, and a fair statement of his faith.

> 'Come, O come
> With the lonely lust of devildom.
> Thrust the sword through the galling fetter,
> All devourer all begetter:
> Give me the sign of the Open Eye
> And the token erect of thorny thigh
> And the word of madness and mystery,
> O Pan, Io Pan!'

The City of New York was not, even in the early years of the present century, a suitable locale for Pantheistic worship. Indeed; when Crowley consulted a hexagram as to the best place to go to found his increasingly more urgently desired community, back came the answer—'Cefalú could not be better.'

And so to Sicily he went. The 'abbey' was by no means all that Crowley could have wished. His original grandiose plan— involving pillars and a domed roof of glass—had to be abandoned; the manager of the Italian bank to whom Crowley applied for a loan proving unconvinced of the financial soundness of the proposition. The building with which the Great Beast had ultimately to be content was much more modest: an ordinary villa in fact; although he named it 'The Abbey of

Thelema'. The central room of this building was used as a Sanctum Sanctorum. On the floor of this the magic circle and pentagram were painted. In the centre of the former stood a six-sided altar. Obscene paintings decorated the walls of this, as of the other rooms of the house. In the altar were kept the 'Cakes of Light', the recipe for which included, amongst other things; meal, honey, red wine and olive oil ('afterwards soften and smooth down with rich, fresh blood'). The *Sunday Express* later hinted at still more debased and unpalatable ingredients.

Crowley's daily intake of heroin was, by this time, absolutely prodigious. But his constitution and brain remained unaffected, and he succeeded in writing, in an extraordinarily short space of time (averaging nearly five thousand words a day) his 'Diary of a Drug Fiend'. This work he dictated to 'my Scarlet Woman of whoredom' and finished it inside of a month, in spite of a mysterious fever contracted during the last week.

Naturally the book did not pass unnoticed.

In the *Sunday Express* of 19 November, 1922, James Douglas, a leading journalist of the 'twenties, launched enthusiastically into the attack, with the avowed intention of obtaining a prosecution. After discussing, briefly, the undesirability of providing free publicity for pornographic literature by review-ing it, he concludes that it is much more important that the hatred of all right-thinking people should be brought down upon the head of the villainous author. This satisfactory decision having been reached, he is free to start on the real stuff.

'It is a novel describing the orgies of vice practised by a group of moral degenerates who stimulate their degraded lusts by doses of cocaine and heroin,' and he quotes triumphantly, out of context, such sentences as: 'Until you have got your mouth full of cocaine you don't know what kissing is.' As might be expected, he utterly rejects the possibility that the motives of the Thelemites can be anything other than crude and unbridled lust.

216

This was only the beginning for next week Crowley was on the front page:

'COMPLETE EXPOSURE OF "DRUG-FIEND" AUTHOR'

read the headlines.

'The man Aleister Crowley is the organizer of societies for pagan orgies.'

'He engaged in pro-German propaganda during the war.'

'He published obscene attacks on the King.'

The *Sunday Express* claimed to have interviewed one of Crowley's female 'victims'. Their information, such of it as can be checked, seems to tally with the known facts. The woman interviewed is believed to have been Mary Butts, a visitor to Cefalú. From her they learned that Crowley had put up pictures, 'unspeakably vile things, depicting antique orgies and dreadful vices.'

The Sanctum Sanctorum is then described, and here, says the *Sunday Express*, 'are carried on unspeakable orgies, impossible of description . . . suffice it to say that they are horrible beyond the misgivings of decent people.'

Crowley has a flock of betrayed but adoring women constantly in attendance, and these, when the abbey is short of funds, are sent out soliciting on the streets of Palermo and Naples. His books are: 'either incomprehensible or disgusting, generally both.'

The accusations of the *Sunday Express* were not, it must be admitted, completely without foundation. Ascetism was supposed to play a part in the ceremonies and daily ritual at Cefalú, particularly in the case of new disciples. Crowley's demands for periods of silence, work and meditation were so exorbitant that they were seldom if ever adhered to by the newly-converted. The 'Eleusinian Mysteries' of the abbey always proved more agreeable to visitors than the ascetic element of the worship.

Nobody could deny that the Great Beast had a magnetic personality, and there was no difficulty in obtaining a supply of suitably awe-inspired pupils. It was the visit, ending in disaster, of one of these, which provided the Beaverbrook press with further meat on which to chew.

To Crowley's need for disciples, the person of Raoul Loveday was the ideal answer. This clever, but rather unbalanced young man, married, whilst still an undergraduate, Betty May, an artists' model with a stormy past and a violent temper: the 'Tiger Woman' of her own autobiography. However, as she had constant cause to complain, he was more devoted to magic than to her. It was inevitable that in the course of his explorations he should sooner or later meet Crowley, and when he did so he was instantly and fatally magnetized, just as from the first Betty was repelled and antagonized.

Crowley, recognizing in Loveday somebody whom he could mould to his purpose, issued an invitation to the abbey. This was instantly accepted by Raoul, although Betty, to whom Epstein had said that: 'If you go, one of you will never return,' was prejudiced against the visit from the start.

After a hideously uncomfortable trans-continental trek by third-class railway compartment; during which Betty was compelled by Loveday to sell her wedding ring; an incident which gave her further cause for resentment and jealousy; they arrived sweating and exhausted at the abbey.

The door was flung open, and before them stood Crowley, clad in his ceremonial robes, intoning theatrically: 'Do what thou wilt shall be the whole of the law.' Admittance was refused the rebellious Betty until she had made the response: 'Love is the law, love under will.'

Inside the abbey, the Beast ruled with a rod of iron. His women had to dye their hair alternately crimson and black. The verbal use of the first person singular was prohibited, and punished by self-inflicted wounds. Drugs lay about the house. Even Crowley's son, aged five, was an addict. This child remarked to the outraged Betty: 'You must leave me alone! I am Beast number two, and can shatter you!'

The daily ritual of the abbey began at dawn with a chant to

Ra, the sun-god. 'Hail unto thee, who art Ra in thy rising.'
In the evening the inmates were expected to attend 'Pentagram'.

The food was disgusting and inadequate; the sanitation non-
existent. Betty May was, by her own account, loud in her
complaints. Crowley had told her that she was now 'Sister
Sybilline' and under the rules of his establishment. She utterly
refused to comply with his requirements, although in order to
obtain admittance at all she had signed a statement saying
that she would do so. One day, whilst waiting on him at table
under protest, she threw a basin of water over his head. He
stirred not a hair; or rather (since he had now shaved himself
as bald as a coot), he moved not a muscle, but a few days
later, quietly took a large knife from a drawer, remarking in a
matter-of-fact voice: 'We shall sacrifice Sister Sybilline at
eight o'clock tonight.' It seemed, moreover, that he was not
joking. In any case, Betty got the wind up sufficiently to nip
out of the house and hide in the mountains (where she nearly
died of exposure) until she thought the danger was past.

By the time she returned, the Beast had transferred his
homicidal desires to a cat. This unfortunate animal, which Betty
attempted to save by smuggling it away into the mountains,
but which returned, apparently eager for death, within a few
hours, was sacrificed, very incompetently, in the Sanctum
Sanctorum.

Crowley had hypnotized it to make it keep still, and when
the ceremony was due to begin it was safely encased in a small
bag. The 'Ape of Thoth', Crowley's current Scarlet Woman,
stood holding the 'Cup of Abominations' ready to catch the
escaping blood. But Loveday, who had been entrusted with
the act of sacrifice, over-excited by the atmosphere and by
large and unaccustomed doses of drugs, struck impulsively, and
too lightly. The cat, bleeding and screaming, writhed from his
grasp and ran yowling round the room. Eventually the enraged
Beast captured and anaesthetized the animal, the precious
blood was caught in the Cup and ceremoniously consumed.

A few days later Loveday went down with enteric fever.

Betty May decided that the disease was due to cat's blood and drugs. In fact he more probably contracted it by drinking water (against the express advice of the Beast), at a monastery in the mountains which he and Crowley had visited a few days earlier. The latter now remarked calmly that he thought Loveday would die on 16th February, and so, as it turned out, he did.

Betty May had had enough. She fled from the abbey, first to the British Consul at Palermo, then back to England, where she poured her story into the attentive ear of a reporter from the *Sunday Express*.

The use to which this paper put her information can be readily imagined.

Betty was quoted as saying that the description of the rites of the abbey printed in the earlier articles were a gross understatement of the true facts.

Loveday (who was not mentioned by name), had been lured by false promises into 'a maelstrom of filth and obscenity.'

And as for the children! 'They are made to witness horrible sexual debauches unbelievably revolting.' The article ended with an invitation to Crowley to sue.

He did not sue. The days of the abbey were drawing to a close. More and more rumours had been escaping from Cefalú. Two earlier visitors to the abbey had returned with stories of the Scarlet Woman ceremonially copulating with a goat, the animal being sacrificed at the moment of climax so that its blood flowed in torrents over her white and naked back. This information had been given to the *Sunday Express* by Mary Butts, who provided the material for the earlier articles, but they apparently considered it too hot to use.

The Beast stated openly that he had: 'driven (himself) to delight in dirty and disgusting debauches.'

Shortly after the Loveday incident he received a 'request', politely but uncompromisingly phrased, to leave Italian territory immediately.

'All of us?' demanded the appalled and heartbroken Beast. Solemnly and apologetically the Chief of Police nodded his head. Despairing the Beast departed. The days of his greatest magic were gone for ever.

In 1922 and 1923 Crowley had declined, perhaps wisely, to sue the *Sunday Express* for libel. In 1934 he decided, undoubtedly unwisely, to sue Nina Hamnett, once his friend, for a single paragraph which appeared in her book *Laughing Torso*. Speaking of the temple at Cefalú she had written: 'He was supposed to practise Black Magic there, and one day a baby was said to have disappeared mysteriously. There was also a goat there. This all pointed to Black Magic, so people said, and the inhabitants of the village were frightened of him.'

Why Crowley decided to sue as a result of this comparatively innocuous paragraph it is impossible to imagine. The defence of Miss Hamnett, of her publishers and of her printers, was, as might have been easily foreseen: justification.

Crowley's attitude was that he was certainly a magician, but white, not black. That was the suggestion that he particularly objected to.

Asked to explain the difference between black and white magic, Crowley replied that magic was the moulding of external circumstances in accordance with the will. If the will was good, the magic was white; if evil, black.

Unfortunately, a formidable array of evidence was produced against him, largely composed of his own inverted boasting.

'Did you say: "Horatio Bottomley branded me as a dirty, degenerate cannibal"?' asked learned counsel; and Crowley answered 'yes'.

Betty May gave evidence for several hours, apparently undismayed by attempts to discredit her. (To the question: 'How many times have you been married?' she replied: 'I think four times.')

She repeated her stories of abbey life, although rather incoherently. 'There was a sort of hysterical business. They called on gods. There was an invocation. There was an enormous painting in the room.'

'What was it like?'—'Terrible.'

'Do you mean indecent?'—'Most.'

The counsel representing the three defendants did not lose the unlimited opportunities afforded them for the exercise of schoolboy wit. Crowley was invited to make himself or learned counsel disappear. (Here the judge intervened.) He was questioned about his numerous aliases.

'Did you take to yourself the designation of "The Beast 6 6 6"?'

' "The Beast 6 6 6" only means "sunlight", you can call me "Little Sunshine." ' (Laughter in court.)

Finally Mr. Justice Swift, who had been becoming more and more glassy-eyed, held up his hand and addressed the jury.

'I have been over forty years engaged in the administration of the law in one capacity or another. I thought that I knew of every conceivable form of wickedness. I thought that everything which was vicious and bad had been produced at one time or another before me. I have learnt in this case that we can always learn something more if we live long enough. I have never heard such dreadful, horrible, blasphemous, and abominable stuff as that which has been produced by the man who describes himself as the greatest living poet. Are you still of the same mind, or do you want the case to go on?'

The jury found for the defendants without leaving the court.

In spite of this tremendous tribute Crowley's days of magic were over. At the end of his life he was reduced to peddling (admittedly at exorbitant rates), a sort of elixir-to-cure-all-ills of his own invention, called 'Amrita'.

In the issue reporting the last day of the action, the *Daily Mail* carried an article claiming that Crowley was by no means the only practitioner of the Black Arts. There were, it claimed, witch-cults scattered over the length and breadth of England.

'These ceremonies have a demoralizing effect on the

witnesses. Lights are lowered, incense is burned in large quantities on a species of altar from behind which hidden "disciples" chant. English, Latin, gibberish are chanted by the hierophant (or "priest") as he demonstrates the "sacred" mysteries. Often the effect is added to by the whirling of what is known in Australia as a "bull-roarer"—an instrument which emits a low, moaning drone, the continuous vibrations of which are calculated to provoke nervous hysteria. Usually prayers are offered to; "Lord Satan, Asmodeus, Beelzebub, Lord of the World". What follows the climax of the ceremony is too abominable for description.'

Crowley died on 1 December, 1947. He was cremated at Brighton Crematorium four days later. At the ceremony the Hymn to Pan was chanted by the faithful few. Scandalized protests to and by the Council followed this incident. Finally the chairman of the Crematorium announced that 'we shall take all necessary steps to prevent such an incident occurring again'!

There does not really seem to be much danger of quite so extravagant an incident occurring again. Crowley lived seventy-two years, throughout which he devoted himself with obvious sincerity to his magical practices. The witch-cult still lives in 'civilized' Europe, but it does so furtively, and with less glorious and exotic trappings than those of the Thelemites. Not many men have the inclination or patience to carry their games so far, and anyway, in Crowley's case it was not a game.

If we compare the life of a roughly contemporaneous and apparently similar figure, we get a different impression, and realize the extent to which Crowley was unique.

Gregory Efimovitch 'Rasputin' was born of humble parents at a village called Petronovskoye in Siberia, in the year 1871. His father evidently possessed some of the qualities which later characterized his son, for the word 'rasputny' means in Russian 'debauched'.

In 1904 Gregory Efimovitch joined a religious sect known as

'Khlysty', the motto of which seems to have been; 'sin that you may be forgiven.' This clearly appealed to Rasputin, for, within a comparatively short space of time, he had gathered round him an adoring group of female catamites. With these he held what he was pleased to call 'sacrificial prayer-meetings.' These meetings have been described by 'the inhabitants of Petronovskoye'—a description quoted by Vogel-Jørgensen.

'At night, when the stars appear in the sky, Rasputin with his household and adherents of both sexes make excursions into the woods. They pile up firewood and kindle a pyre. On a tripod set on the fire is placed a vessel with incense and herbs. Men and women join hands and form a ring round the pyre, dance, and sing continuously and monotonously this single verse:

> "Our sin is for repentance sake,
> For penitence our sin O God."

The dance round the fire grows quicker and quicker, wilder and wilder; sighs and groans are heard; the fire goes out, and, in the ensuing darkness, Rasputin's voice is heard exclaiming: "Try your flesh."

All fling themselves on the ground, then the confusion becomes general, and a shameless orgy begins.'

Rasputin's creed, as stated by himself, was this: 'a particle of the Supreme Being is incarnated in me. Only through me you can hope to be saved; and the manner of your salvation is this: you must be united with me in soul and *body*.' (Italics mine.)

A rather crude religion: not thought out in any detail, and an occasional pin-prick of anxiety seems to have afflicted some of the worshippers. One of Rasputin's girls once enquired with naive anxiety: 'But Gregory Efimovitch, isn't what we do with you sinful?' To which he reassuringly if inconsistently replied: 'No, my child, it is not sin: our flesh is from God, and we can freely employ it.'

This answer seems to be in direct contradiction to the main

tenet of the creed. But what Rasputin lacked in consistency, he made up by the hypnotic overwhelmingness of his manner and dress; and it was not surprising that he should soon turn his talents to finer material.

During a visit to St. Petersburg he met the Archimandrite, who, fascinated by his personality and moved by the tale, doubtless dramatically told and suitably censored, of his 'conversion' and religious activities, presented him at court.

The opportunity was not lost on Gregory Efimovitch. However big a charlatan he may have been as regards the sincerity of his 'beliefs', personal qualities of some kind he undoubtedly possessed, even though they seem to have affected women rather than men. His uncouth appearance and manner, instead of proving a handicap, acted rather as an added attraction.

At meals, when he had finished eating (which he did with his fingers) 'he puts out his hands to his lady admirers, who belong to the very highest nobility, and makes them lick his fingers clean, a duty they perform with gratitude, not to say devotion.'

This cornering of the ladies of the Russian court, apart from the political influence which it enabled him to exercise, naturally made him enemies. He provided them with plenty of potential ammunition, and this they did not hesitate to make actual.

Rasputin, although normally filthy in his habits, had no objection to taking a bath, as long as everybody else in the bath-house was female. Von Zanka described (source not mentioned) a religious meeting held by Rasputin in the house of a lady from Marseilles known as 'Madame Discretion'.

Five ladies arrived in sleighs, entering first the house, and then the bath. (The Russian bath is something like a Turkish bath.)

'Gregory Efimovitch is already there. It is very hot inside, quite 104 degrees Fahrenheit. When Father Grishka sees his faithful assembled he begins to preach. He speaks with consider-

able animation, for, as we have said before, it is very hot, and
Father Grishka has much with which his tender-loving heart
is brimming over. Father Grishka gesticulates and bellows. In
glowing colours he paints the lures of sin and the bane of the
flesh. His audience hangs with burning eyes on his lips, and, as
we have said before, it is very hot. Their pulses throb, and the
heat makes the faithful almost faint; but the preacher becomes
still more excited by the awful temperature. Still more vividly
he depicts how all mankind, without exception, is fallen a prey
to sin and vice and crimes. . . . The congregation is soon
bewitched by this glowing eloquence. . . . The prophet's eyes
are aflame. Ah! vice is dreadful, and the flesh is enemy to the
spirit. Why has God in His wisdom made the temptations of
the flesh irresistible? The audience cannot answer. The temperature rises and the audience are in a corresponding condition
of fervour on account of the heat and Father Grishka's burning
words. But if the sin is great, yet vastly much greater is the
sinner's forgiveness. When he reaches this point, Father
Grishka is in a state of ecstasy: his voice sticks fast to his
throat: he talks with his tongue. The audience snorts and gasps
while the heat becomes more and more intense. . . .'

But such was the personality of the man, that the spreading
of such reports, true as they undoubtedly were, was not enough.
They may well have had exactly the opposite effect from that
intended. Guards of honour would continue to meet him at
railway stations; his name would continue to be breathed with
reverent awe in all the drawing-rooms of Russia. Looking at
the photographs of this shaggy-faced charlatan, it is hard to
conceive what can have been his attraction. The attitude of all
who met him was as towards a being from another world.
Only murder could get rid of him, and even this nearly failed.

A group led by Prince Yusupoff and the Grand Duke
Dimitri Pavlovitch laid the plot. Cakes were stuffed with
crystals of potassium cyanide. The same poison was smeared
inside a wine-glass. Rasputin was invited to come and see the
Prince. He came round, dressed in one of his exotic outfits.

(He sometimes wore a blouse of pale blue silk with velvet trousers. On this occasion the blouse was embroidered with cornflowers.) Yusupoff had been entrusted with the entertaining and poisoning of Rasputin. The latter, after at first surlily refusing the cakes on the grounds that they were too sweet, finally gobbled them all up one after the other. Each of them contained enough poison to kill an ordinary man. Yusupoff, greatly relieved, sat back to await results. None came. After a while the Prince offered Rasputin some poisoned Madeira. This he drank slowly, sipping it thoughtfully 'like a connoisseur.' A few minutes later he complained of a slight irritation in the throat and asked for more wine. Still no effect. Yusupoff on the other hand, was almost ready to faint. Rasputin asked the Prince to sing. He complied in a quavering voice. Rasputin still showed signs of only slight discomfort. Leaving the room as steadily as he could, Yusupoff obtained a revolver from his confederates, and returning, shot Rasputin through the heart. 'There was a roar as from a wild beast, and Rasputin fell heavily backwards on the bearskin rug.' The Prince called his friends. Rushing in they saw Rasputin lying apparently dead on the floor.

A few moments later, whilst they were making preparations to dispose of the body, Rasputin suddenly came to life again. His left eye slowly opened in a terrifying leer. Reeling to his feet, he rushed at Yusupoff with eyes crossed and fingers knotted. 'The room resounded with a wild roar.' Foam drooled from the corners of his mouth. In a hoarse whisper he repeated Yusupoff's name.

The Prince escaped his demoniac clutches, and called to his friends for the revolver. By the time it arrived Rasputin was crawling up the stairs on all fours. Four times more they shot him, and finally he fell, and lay motionless. Then he stirred again. In a frenzy of rage and terror the Prince battered in his head with a loaded cane. Such was the electric vitality of the man who had fascinated the court of Russia.

Although the disquiet of the present age seems to be due to

or, at any rate, connected with what I have described as a sort of mental agoraphobia, the move towards sexual liberty has not yet reached its limit, and certainly there are some people who still feel the need for restraint.

The important fact about the sexual restraint of the modern type is that it comes from within, not from without. It is, of course, preferable in every way to the neurosis-based 'self-control' of the middle ages.

The more one thinks about the number and nature of people exercising restraint of this kind, the more one wonders whether the present swing of the pendulum will ever be completed. (I am not implying that the return swing may not be made, but that each swing will grow shorter.) People have begun to see some of the dangers of liberty; they have already seen those of restriction.

These dangers everybody interprets differently. Some in the light of the clerics who strenuously resisted all attempts at condoning the Feast of Fools, but others, and an increasing number of others, with greater self-insight and perspicacity. The results of these mental processes, although similar, are very far from identical; and it is something to be grateful for that restraints of the medieval kind are on the wane, and, in inverse ratio, restraints caused by more natural impulses on the increase.

There is more to be grateful for than that. We are at the moment in a period of balance, and for once the human race seems to be considering pulling the communication cord, and going for a walk on the platform. What the result of this experiment, if indeed it is taking place, will be, it is too early to decide.

But much progress has already been made. Human beings are developing self-insight, and a realization of the need for a system of self-insight, and for a system of self-control as carefully organized and maintained as their motor-cars and railway services.

To strike the balance between innocence and knowledge is our problem.

To say that we were approaching as sane an outlook on life as the ancient Greeks, or even that we were consciously attempting to do so, would be going too far. But the shuddering away from the huge vistas spread before us by, for example, the development of nuclear fission (the shuddering very reasonable in this case), *could* be interpreted as a move, perhaps an unconscious one, towards the naïvety of the Hellenic world, an attempt to regain our innocence which is lost.

Sexual *guilt* has left most of us, but this has not resulted in an outbreak of general debauchery of the kind seen during the Renaissance period. We see rather a kind of cheerfully self-imposed restraint in the choice of day-to-day behaviour. In these circumstances, one would expect to find examples of the periodic outlets of sexual feeling that we saw in ancient Greece.

'Petting-parties' are essentially unique to the twentieth century. Kinsey, Pomeroy and Martin: '*Sexual Behaviour in the Human Male*' say; speaking of this form of sexual activity:

'During the past few decades, particularly at upper social levels, premarital physical contacts between males and females have been considerably elaborated without any increase in the frequency of actual intercourse. These contacts may go far beyond the hugging and kissing which occurred in older generations. In their maximum extension they may include all of the techniques of the pre-coital play in which sophisticated married partners engage.'

The important feature of this form of activity is that it provides an *emotional* outlet, as well as a physical (climax being reached by masturbation). There is none of the 'holding back' practised during the Victorian period. It should be remembered that those practising petting are unmarried.

Although an emotional purge takes place, and although the presence of other human beings gives the impression of being borne along on a tide of common emotion, with a corresponding sense of lack of personal responsibility (provided in the ancient world by assuming the existance of a deity), full catharsis is absent.

This is not true of another twentieth-century activity, in which, however, the emotional outlet, although violent, is less consciously sexual.

In all ancient cults involving sexuality, an important feature of the deity in the eyes of the worshipper is his impersonality. Not, of course, that the deity does not have an extremely powerful *individuality*, but he is remote, as visible but as untouchable as the sun and the moon. However violently he may affect the lives of men, he will always remain remote and untouchable. Thus; at one time in the history of Roman religion a bride, before entering her husband's bed, squatted on the wooden phallus of Mutunus Tutunus, a deity who represented in the abstract, the whole of male sexuality.

Part of the purpose, conscious or unconscious, of this action, was that the bride, if she was a virgin, should feel no personal resentment against her husband for the pain of defloration. Somehow the remoteness, the impersonality of the deity made it easier for her, made the transition from chastity to married life more gradual. The first man to possess her was man in the abstract.

At the beginning of the century, or soon after it, young people of both sexes worshipped film stars. Now a new form of worship has appeared and quite recently, in the shape of a sequence of new varieties of music forms—skiffle, rock-and-roll, etc., which, particularly in the case of the latter, involve a rhythm and movement which individually, but more particularly in combination, produce an impression suggestive in the extreme. The 'deities' of this new cult appear to be exclusively male, the outlet being provided for members of the opposite sex. The surplus energies of the males seem to be exuded in different forms, sometimes in activity punishable under the criminal law.

As at all periods when some form of 'police-control' is not in use to control the morality, or rather the immorality, of the people, fairs and public holidays are frequently made the occasion for debauchery; one of the essential ideas behind the orgy being present—that what is done on that day 'does not count' it does not go down on the record. The Mardi Gras celebrations in the United States, in particular, are said to lead to openly indecent behaviour—or rather to behaviour which at other times would be considered indecent. Other countries have equivalents, the Fasching in Germany being only one example; none of them in any basic respect different from the feast days of the ancients (except for the absence of a deity). Sometimes, of course, a kind of 'anti-deity' is present in the minds of the normally religious: the idea that they are rebelling temporarily against the person or concept of God. (As in the case of the priests and the Feast of Fools.)

In the present age there are many who have no need for the orgy. There are still more who think they do not need it; but people are learning to come to a reckoning with themselves and with their consciences. The discoveries of the psychologists have made big changes to our outlook on life, and particularly, to our outlook on sexuality. We can no longer escape responsibility for our actions now that we know the truth. Knowledge cannot be wiped out.

Even so, the orgy principle has its advantages. Some of these I defined in the preface. Change is essential to all of us. No gourmet would think of eating his favourite dish for breakfast, lunch, dinner and tea. No one in his senses will devote his life entirely to sexual indulgence, nor will he renounce it altogether. Even if people no longer fear the wrath of the gods, they still fear the contempt of their friends and the pricking of their own conscience, and from ordinary temperance it is well to have an escape; particularly if this escape can somehow be placed outside the rules of ordinary morality. Some people will, realizing the truth of these precepts, continue to feel it imperative to create, if they do not already believe in, some external influence over their actions. To these, denying their own responsibility, and rejecting the dubious wisdom of the scientific age, will the orgy continue to be a possibility and a necessity.

SELECTED BIBLIOGRAPHY

Athenaeus of Nanclia: The Deipnosophists or: *The Banquet of the Learned.* Translated G. B. Gulick. Heinemann, 1927.

AUBREY, J.: *Brief Lives.* Cresset Press, 1949.

BACKMAN, E. L.: *Religious Dances in the Christian Church.* Allen and Unwin, 1952.

Beeton's Christmas Annual, 1873.

BLOCH, IWAN: *Sexual Life in England.* Aldor, 1938.

BREND, W. A.: *Sacrifice to Attis: a Study of Sex and Civilization.* Heinemann, 1931.

BURCHARD, JOHN: *Diary.* (No full English translation available.)

BURCKHARDT, J.: *The Civilization of the Renaissance in Italy.* Phaidon Press, 1937.

BURDY, S.: *Life of Philip Skelton.* Dublin, 1792.

CASANOVA DI SEINGALT, GIACOMO GIROLAMO: *Memoirs.* Translated Arthur Machen. Casanova Society, 1922.

CHAMBERS, E. K.: *The Medieval Stage.* Clarendon Press, 1903.

CHANCELLOR, E. BERESFORD: *Lives of the Rakes.* Philip Allan, 1925.

CRUMP, C. G. and JACOB, E. F.: *The Legacy of the Middle Ages.* Clarendon Press, 1926.

DE BEAUVOIR, S.: *Le Deuxième Sexe.* Gallimard, 1949.

DELASSUS, J.: *Les Incubes et les Succubes.* Paris, 1897.

DU TILLOT, L.: *Memories pour servir a l'histoire de la fête des fous.* Lausanne, 1741.

ELLIS, H. HAVELOCK.: *Psychology of Sex.* Heinemann, 1933.

ELLIS, H. HAVELOCK: *Sex in Relation to Society.* Davis, 1910.

EVELYN, J.: *Diary,* edited E. S. de Beer. Oxford, 1955.

FARNELL, L. R.: *Cults of the Greek States.* Clarendon Press, 1896.

FREUD, S.: *Collected Papers: Obsessive Acts and Religious Practices.* Hogarth, 1924.

FREUD, S.: *Collected Papers*: *A Neurosis of Demoniacal Possession in the 17th Century*. Hogarth, 1924.

FULLER, R.: *Hell-Fire Francis*. Chatto and Windus, 1939.

GOODLAND, R.: *A Bibliography of Sex Rites and Customs*. Routledge, 1931.

GORER, G.: *The Life and Ideas of the Marquis de Sade*. Owen, 1953.

GUTHRIE, W. K. C.: *The Greeks and their Gods*. Methuen, 1950.

HEINE, M.: *Marquis de Sade*. Paris, 1950.

HOLTBY, W.: *Women in a Changing Civilization*. Bodley Head, 1939.

JOHNSTON, C.: *Chrysal*. 1785.

JONES, LOUIS C.: *The Clubs of the Georgian Rakes*. Columbia University Press, 1942.

KIEFER, OTTO: *Sexual Life in Ancient Rome*. Routledge and Kegan Paul, 1934.

KINSEY, A., and others: *Sexual Behaviour in the Human Male*. W. B. Saunders, 1948.

KINSEY, A., and others: *Sexual Behaviour in the Human Female*. W. B. Saunders, 1953.

KNIGHT, R. P.: *An account of the Remains of the Worship of Priapus*. London, 1786.

LANE, J.: *Puritan Rake and Squire*. Evans, 1950.

LEA, H. C.: *A History of Sacerdotal Celibacy in the Christian Church*. Williams and Norgate, 1907.

LICHT, H.: *Sexual Life in Ancient Greece*. Routledge and Kegan Paul.

MARAÑON, G.: *Tiberio*. Buenos Aires, 1942.

MAY, G.: *Social Control of Sexual Expression*. Allen and Unwin, 1930.

MOMENTI, P. G.: *Venice*. Murray, 1907.

MURRAY, M.: *The God of the Witches*. Sampson Low, 1933.

MURRAY, M.: *The Witch Cult in Western Europe*. Clarendon Press, 1921.

PEARL, C.: *The Girl with the Swansdown Seat*. Muller, 1955.

PEPYS, S.: *Diary*. Edited Wheatley. George Bell, 1904.

PRAZ, M.: *The Romantic Agony*. Milford, 1933.

QUINLAN, M. J.: *Victorian Prelude*. Columbia University Press, 1949.

ROSENBAUM, J.: *Historie de la Syphilis dans l'antiquité*. Bruxelles, 1847.

RYAN, M.: *Prostitution in London*. Baillère, 1839.

SAVAGE, H.: *The Harleian Miscellany*. Palmer, 1924.

SCOT, R.: *The Discoverie of Witchcraft*. Rodke, 1930.

SKELTON, P.: *The Complete Works of R. Boyne*. 1824.

STEKEL, W.: *Sadism and Masochism*. London. 1935.

STUBBES, P.: *The Anatomie of Abuses*. 1583.

SYMONDS, J.: *The Great Beast*. Rider, 1951.

TAYLOR, GORDON RATTRAY: *Sex in History*. Thames and Hudson, 1953.

VOGEL-JØRGENSEN: *Rasputin*. T. Fisher Unwin, 1917.

WARD, E.: *The Secret History of Clubs*. 1709.

WALPOLE, H.: *Memoirs of the reign of George III*.

WALPOLE, H.: *Journals of Visits to Country Seats*. Walpole Society, 1928.

WELSFORD, E.: *The Fool: his Social and Literary History*. Faber, 1935.

YUSUPOFF, PRINCE: *Rasputin*. Jonathan Cape, 1927.

Dictionary of National Biography.

Hell upon Earth: or the Town in an Uproar. 1729.

New Foundling Hospital For Wit.

Nocturnal Revels: or the History of the King's Place.

The Hellfire Club, kept by a Society of Blasphemers. 1721.

The Irish Blasters, or the Votaries of Bacchus. Dublin, 1738.

Records of the Most Ancient and Puissant Order of the Beggar's Benison and Merryland Anstruther. Privately printed, 1892.

The Town and Country Magazine.

INDEX

INDEX

239